beating
eating disorders
Step by Step

of related interest

Inside Anorexia
Stories from Girls and their Families
Christine Halse, Anne Honey and Desiree Boughtwood
ISBN 978 1 84310 597 8

In and Out of Anorexia
The Story of the Client, the Therapist and the Process of Recovery
Tammie Ronen and Ayelet
ISBN 978 1 85302 990 5

Anorexics on Anorexia
Edited by Rosemary Shelley
ISBN 978 1 85302 471 9

The Overweight Patient
A Psychological Approach to Understanding and Working with Obesity
Kathy Leach
ISBN 978 1 84310 366 0

Drawing from Within
Using Art to Treat Eating Disorders
Lisa D. Hinz
ISBN 978 1 84310 822 1

A Systemic Treatment of Bulimia Nervosa
Women in Transition
Carole Kayrooz
Foreword by a Service User
ISBN 978 1 85302 918 9

Bulimia Nervosa
A Cognitive Therapy Programme for Clients
Myra Cooper, Gillian Todd and Adrian Wells
ISBN 978 1 85302 717 8

Living with Emetophobia
Coping with Extreme Fear of Vomiting
Nicolette Heaton-Harris
Foreword by Linda Dean
ISBN 978 1 84310 536 7

By Their Own Young Hand
Deliberate Self-harm and Suicidal Ideas in Adolescents
Keith Hawton and Karen Rodham
With Emma Evans
ISBN 978 1 84310 230 4

Cutting it Out
A Journey through Psychotherapy and Self-harm
Carolyn Smith
Foreword by Maggie Turp
ISBN 978 1 84310 266 3

beating
eating disorders
Step by Step

A Self-Help Guide for Recovery

Anna Paterson

Jessica Kingsley Publishers
London and Philadelphia

First published in 2008
by Jessica Kingsley Publishers
116 Pentonville Road
London N1 9JB, UK
and
400 Market Street, Suite 400
Philadelphia, PA 19106, USA

www.jkp.com

Library of Congress Cataloging in Publication Data
Paterson, Anna, 1968-
 Beating eating disorders step by step : a self-help guide for recovery / Anna Paterson.
     p. cm.
 ISBN 978-1-84310-340-0 (pb : alk. paper) 1. Eating disorders--Treatment. I. Title.
 RC552.E18P38 2008
 616.85'2606--dc22
                                    2007033190

British Library Cataloguing in Publication Data
A CIP catalogue record for this book is available from the British Library

ISBN 978 1 84310 340 0

Printed and bound in the United States by
Thomson-Shore, Inc.

Thank you to Simon who changed my life in such a wonderful way; thank you also for your constant support and invaluable help with all aspects of my work, including editing the books.

I would also like to thank my mother-in-law, Cherry, for her continual kindness, warmth and humour.

Contents

Introduction: My Story — 9

1: What are Eating Disorders? — 15

2: Choosing Recovery — 28

3: Letting Go of Your Illness — 44

4: Coping with Guilt — 58

5: Writing a Thoughts and Feelings Diary — 67

6: Cognitive Behaviour Therapy — 72

7: Exposure Therapy — 86

8: Triggers and How to Deal with Them — 91

9: Dysfunctional Beliefs — 103

10: How to Stop Dangerous Behaviours — 113

11: Anger Management — 127

12: Anxiety Management — 137

13: Assertiveness Training — 146

14: Perfectionism — 158

15: Building Confidence — 167

16: Living at a Healthy Weight — 173

17: Coping with Setbacks — 184

18: Recipes for a Positive Approach to Food — 190

Conclusion: The Jigsaw Approach to Recovery — 212

USEFUL RESOURCES — 213

INDEX — 216

Introduction: My Story

It is likely that my life would have been very different if I had been born a boy. My grandmother liked her grandsons but not her new granddaughter. The abuse began at the age of three and it continued throughout my life at regular intervals.

I was the kind of child that always wanted to please. I was quiet, studious and (as my mother said) a 'very obedient' little girl. I was a perfect victim and I can still instantly recall the torment I endured during my early years. Throughout my childhood I frequently looked after my mother, who suffered from migraines and would often spend time in bed. On those days, I would cook and clean as well as try to protect her from my grandmother (her mother). My father worked in London and had to leave the house by 6.30 each morning, not returning until 6.30 at night. Until the age of 21 (when my father retired) my life was dominated and controlled by my grandmother and mother.

At 13 years old, I was attending the local grammar school. I was achieving good grades and was a member of the hockey and swimming teams. However, years of consistent abuse had left me exhausted. I collapsed at school one day during the autumn term and was not able to move from my bed for three months. I was diagnosed with a virus, although by the time we reached Christmas that year I had started to improve and was ready to return to school in January.

However, my doctor diagnosed depression and gave me antidepressant drugs. When there was no change in my state of mind (which was caused by the abuse rather than the virus) the doses were increased until I was taking a higher dosage than many adults were prescribed. Gradually the drugs began to affect me and I started to hallucinate. These hallucinations became more frequent until I saw them on every blank wall or white page of a book. The words seemed to merge on the page and sentences became unreadable.

Even though I told the doctors about my problems immediately, it was still a few days before the drugs were stopped. By then the condition seemed permanent. Over the next few months I slowly taught myself to read again with the aid of a small piece of card that isolated a few words at a time. For the next couple of years I had to use this card to read and write everything, and it was by using this device that I took all my 'O' level examinations. It wasn't until I reached my 'A' levels (two years later) that I was able to read normally again.

During these difficult teenage years I lost significant amounts of weight on occasions and the words 'anorexia nervosa' were mentioned, but I managed to regain a normal size before any treatment was discussed.

At the age of 17, though, my life began to change dramatically. Serious family problems led to my parents becoming emotionally distant from myself and from each other and my grandmother's influence grew predominant again. My self-esteem dropped dramatically and I believed that everything bad that happened was my fault. I did not think that anyone loved me and wanted to just disappear. As a response, I stopped eating. I had begun to self-harm occasionally at the age of 12 and this now became a regular occurrence since I felt that I deserved to be punished.

Over the next four years, my weight dropped steadily. It rose to near-normal levels during the year I spent in London at college but it soon fell once I returned to live at home. At 19 I started work at a solicitor's office. The first three months were fine but then things began to change. The head of the practice (whom I had enjoyed working for) promoted me and my new boss was a bully. The years of abuse had led me to believe that bad treatment was all I deserved. My boss soon recognized this and two years of sexual harassment and bullying followed.

As my self-esteem fell again, my weight began to plummet and, by the age of 21, I was too ill to work. My parents told me that I was ruining their lives and so the guilt I felt was tremendous, although I still could not force myself to eat. By now, eating had become a terrifying prospect for me. My body was starving hungry and so I became obsessed with food. It occupied my thoughts during every waking moment and then I would sleep fitfully with relentless nightmares.

My parents took me to our family doctor, who was shocked by my dramatic weight loss. He sent me to see a psychiatrist at our local hospital. She diagnosed anorexia and told me just to 'Go home and eat'. I felt even more ashamed and alone. I was supposed to visit an occupational therapist, although my first experience of the clinic terrified me and I refused to return. Instead, I began to see a psychiatric nurse who disagreed with the doctor's diagnosis and started to treat me for ME (chronic fatigue syndrome).

By now I was becoming increasingly withdrawn. I wanted to eat to please my parents, although I just could not do this and so I constantly felt a failure. It was at this time I attempted suicide but stopped half-way through since I could not bear to upset my parents further.

Later that same year, at the age of 50, my father retired from his job and we moved to Cornwall for a fresh start away from my grandmother. It did not occur to me to ask the question 'If my parents knew that my grandmother's behaviour was so bad that they needed to escape from it, why had they constantly sent me to stay with her?' It would be another four years, two hospital inpatient stays and six therapists before I began to look at their behaviour.

Just three months after the move I was taken into hospital. My mother had told two visiting junior doctors that I was impossible to cope with and that I should be in a psychiatric hospital. I had been there for one month when the official psychiatrist for my area returned from holiday. He was annoyed that his junior doctors had arranged inpatient care since he believed that this could sometimes be frightening for anorexia sufferers.

He preferred slow treatment supported by continual assistance from the community mental health team. As I had gained six pounds and was now allowed off total bed-rest, he arranged for me to be discharged. I signed a contract agreeing to see a psychiatric nurse every three days and to gain between a half and one pound of weight each week.

When I left hospital, I was certain that I would never allow the anorexia to take control of my life again. However, within two weeks, the harsh internal 'voice' that had previously convinced me I was stupid and hateful had returned. My parents pressed me to eat more and this resulted in my feeling intense guilt. As a response, I began hiding my food. I hated being deceptive and was constantly terrified of being discovered. I began self-harming again and secretly bought a new knife. The cuts were deeper than any I had made before, although I believed that I deserved the pain. I told no one and hid my damaged arms in the long sleeves of my baggy jumpers and shirts.

Gradually my weight began to drop again. Once it had reached a dangerous level the emergency community treatment team was called in and I worked with a psychiatric nurse called Clive on a daily basis. He was exceptionally dedicated and tried to help me with all aspects of the illness. By this time I believed that I was a nuisance to everyone. He tried to encourage me to ask for anything I wanted but I found this impossible and just wanted to disappear. I felt like I took up too much space in the world.

Although I was slowly increasing my diet with Clive's encouragement, my weight was now too low for my body to process solid food. The doctors felt that the best option was an inpatient unit since I was now only hours from death. I was taken to a Priory Hospital 200 miles from my home, where I stayed for the next six months.

The hospital saved my life and boosted my self-esteem. By the end of my stay, every member of the staff knew me and the nurses took me to the city for days out. They arranged for me to have my hair cut at a top salon and I was thrilled by the results. Everyone praised my new look and said that I finally looked like a 25-year-old woman and not a young girl. I started to help run the therapy groups and spent many hours talking with the new patients, trying to encourage and support them.

My weight had improved greatly, although it was still quite low for my height. It was decided that I should go home for a trial period of a month. I returned to Cornwall excited and hopeful for the future. However, my confidence levels quickly began to drop and I grew quieter and more withdrawn. My brother Mark was portrayed as the success of the family and, once again, I felt that my life was worthless.

My mother frequently told doctors and family members that she wanted to live with just her husband. This naturally left me feeling in the way. My father told me that he did not feel the same way though, and on one occasion said, 'It's you who makes my marriage bearable.' I was confused and often caught in the middle, although it was the negative comments that I heard repeatedly in my head. I constantly scanned my parents' faces and tried to read their minds to see if they were upset with me. The anorexia took a firm hold again as I set out to punish myself for being such a 'bad' person.

My therapists urged me to try family therapy. For a year I found excuses since I was terrified of asking my parents to become involved with my treatment. My fears felt justified when I saw their reaction to the initial letter from the health centre. Neither wanted to go to the appointment and they showed their disapproval in different ways. I could see that my father was frightened and this came out as anger. He did try to reassure me that he wanted to help but his actions and behaviour told a different story. My mother focused totally on my brother and his family before the scheduled meetings by placing photos of them in albums and frames. During the sessions, she would talk about how difficult she felt I was to live with. In her eyes, I did everything wrong, from overfilling the freezer and controlling the television viewing schedule to stopping her from seeing her mother.

I explained to the therapists that I tried not to affect my parents in any way. I was certain that the doctors would think that I deliberately wanted to run my parents' lives. It therefore came as shock when I learnt that they understood the situation very clearly. They told me that they knew I was not controlling my parents' lives and that for most of my 28 years, I was actually the one who was being controlled and directed. They could see how hard I tried to please everyone and wanted to teach me how to stand up for myself.

As was the intention, family therapy showed me how our family functioned. My mother even began to talk openly. One day she told me that she did not care how other people felt – she was only concerned with how everything affected her.

I tried to make a life for myself as best I could. I started my own cross-stitch business and passed my driving test. However, I was living a very controlled, timetabled existence following my parents' schedule. At 29, I felt desperately lonely but had resigned myself to the fact that I would always be alone when everything changed. I joined a pen pal club and contacted Simon through the group. We began to write frequently and I learnt that he also suffered from low self-esteem.

I told Simon about the anorexia and expected him to disappear from my life. However, letters soon became lengthy phone calls and we met after five months. Simon showed me unconditional love and a few months later we were engaged. For six months, we travelled between Cornwall and London (where Simon lived) but the times apart became even harder. In January 2000 we decided to live together permanently. We continued to divide our time between London and Cornwall, but gradually found that we were spending more time with Simon's parents in London.

They welcomed me with open arms and I had never felt so loved before. I apologized constantly for being in the way, for making too much noise, for using the wrong plate, and 101 other imaginary things but nothing upset them. They would just smile and say how lucky they were to have me as a daughter-in-law. With their and Simon's love, my recovery moved at a rapid pace. No one watched what I ate or commented on my size – they did not mind so long as I was happy. This freedom was life-changing for me and I started to try all kinds of new foods and gained weight at a slow but steady pace.

As I recovered, I felt that I wanted to try and help other eating disorder sufferers and so wrote my autobiography *Anorexic*. I started to receive many letters from sufferers asking me for tips on recovery and so then I wrote *Diet of Despair* – a self-help book for teenagers and their families. I followed this with

Running on Empty (a novel for young adults) and *Fit to Die* (a self-help book about the growing problem of eating disorders among men). My most recent book, *Just Like Doris Day*, is a novel for young people about bullying.

Through these books and my website (www.annapaterson.com) I hope that I am able to help sufferers to choose recovery and begin to fight back against their own eating disorders.

Chapter 1

What are Eating Disorders?

There are a number of different types of eating disorders, each with their own traits and symptoms. It is likely that you have picked up this workbook because you have (or suspect that you have) an eating disorder. It is hoped that you are now looking into the possibility of recovery.

Eating disorders are difficult and painful illnesses to live with, but frequently sufferers find it hard to take the step of choosing recovery. This is often because the disorder has developed as a way of 'coping' with problems or stresses in the sufferer's life. To beat the disorder, sufferers have to learn new and positive ways of dealing with any difficult issues in their lives.

The three main eating disorders are anorexia nervosa, bulimia nervosa, and compulsive overeating. There is also a fourth – a broader category known as 'eating disorders not otherwise specified' (ED-NOS) which encompasses all the remaining eating-related problems such as bulimarexia, orthorexia and body dysmorphia.

Anorexia nervosa

Anorexia nervosa (literally meaning 'nervous loss of appetite') is the most well-known eating disorder since the appearance of sufferers can be dramatic. The name is misleading, though, since sufferers have not lost their appetite – they are actually controlling it with an iron will. Ignoring hunger pangs, they will refuse food even though they are desperate to eat. They can gain pleasure from losing weight and this feeling of success will spur them on to deny themselves further nutrition.

However, anorexia is not really an illness about food and weight at all – these are just the outward symptoms of deeper problems. The illness concerns sufferers' need to regain some control in a life which has overwhelmed them. Frequently, anorexia sufferers have high expectations of themselves and strive for perfection. They feel terrified at the idea of failing and boost their poor self-esteem by successfully losing weight.

Dieting is universally recognized as difficult and yet anorexia sufferers are capable of denying themselves everything. The complex nature of the illness means that the physical problems (emaciation and malnutrition) are often the first to be observed.

It may only be when sufferers are confronted that they admit to even having a problem. Even when the issue is clearly obvious to friends and relatives, sufferers might deny they are restricting their dietary intake owing to a fear of being made to eat or gain weight. They can become withdrawn and secretive, hiding their emaciated bodies under many layers of baggy clothing.

A doctor will make a medical diagnosis of anorexia if the following symptoms are evident:

- an intense fear of weight gain

- for female sufferers, the cessation of their menstrual period for three consecutive months

- extremely low body weight

- body image distortion and dissatisfaction.

The following is an extract from my own diary, which I kept during my years of anorexia.

Wednesday 20 November 1997

I've been having a really difficult time with food lately and it's getting me down. I know it's not really food that's the problem – that's just the direction into which I've channelled all the unhappiness that's inside of me. The doctor told me that if I can sort out my emotional problems then all the rest will fall into place naturally. If I could just face the underlying causes of my anorexia then I won't 'need' it any longer to protect me. Food will no longer be a problem. That sounds like an impossible state to reach though because I feel so terrified of food right now.

Although anorexia has been reported in both men and women from the ages of 6 to 60, it is still most commonly seen in teenage girls. They tend to be high achievers who are usually closely enmeshed with their family. It is an illness that occurs in all classes and ethnic groups, although it currently remains predominant in white, middle-class families where social and academic achievement is strongly emphasized.

Despite frequently being known as the 'slimmer's disease', it has been estimated that approximately 75 per cent of anorexia sufferers have never been overweight. The illness can develop for many different reasons, including bullying, abuse, family issues, high expectations of academic success, and the death of a loved one. Learning why they initially 'escaped' into their eating disorder is a vital part of sufferers' recovery.

If you are still feeling doubtful as to whether you are suffering from anorexia, look at the following list of questions. If you agree with the majority of them, it is highly possible that you have the disorder and it would be very wise to consult a doctor.

- Do you have an intense fear of gaining weight?

- Do you feel afraid to eat (especially high-calorie foods)?

- Do you restrict your diet? Are you frequently missing meals?

- Do you throw away food when no one is watching?

- Do you think that you look fat even though people have told you that you are thin?

- Do you spend most (if not all) of your time thinking about food?

- Do you watch cookery programmes and cook meals for other people while avoiding the food yourself?

- Do you spend a lot of time looking in the mirror?

- Do you weigh yourself many times each day?

- Do you constantly feel a desperate need to be thinner?

- Do you think that people will only love you if you are thin?

- Do you feel guilty when you eat?

- Do you lie about how much you have eaten to friends and family?

- Do you have certain rules and rituals connected with food and eating?

- Do you keep a regular check on how many calories you eat each day?

- Do you feel a need to punish yourself if you eat more than you feel you are permitted?

- Do you frequently overexercise (usually in secret)?

- Do you feel happy when you lose weight?

- Do you know the calorific value of every food you eat?

- Do you hate the feeling of having a full stomach?

- Do you feel despondent if you gain weight or eat extra food?

- Do you feel physically unwell? (Headaches, fatigue, constipation, muscular aches, and so on.)

- Do you have difficulty sleeping?

- Do you feel a need to complete any work you do perfectly?

- Do you have trouble concentrating?

Please do be aware that everyone is unique. If you cannot relate to many of these questions, you might still have an eating disorder. Remember that the term 'eating disorder' simply refers to having disordered eating patterns and that can take on many different shapes and forms.

Bulimia nervosa

Bulimia nervosa is a condition in which the sufferer binges on large quantities of food (usually high-fat, high-sugar style products). They then suffer intense feelings of guilt and try to dispose of the food through purging (by taking laxatives) or vomiting. Laxatives and diuretics are often taken in large quantities and sufferers also tends to restrict their diet, overexercise, or both.

Although sufferers may appear to be at a normal weight, they are constantly putting their body under tremendous stress. Since sufferers are usually at a healthy weight for their height, the illness may go undetected and undiagnosed for many months or even years.

Feelings of shame at the way in which they rid themselves of food often cause sufferers to become intensely secretive about their disorder. I have heard from young women who travelled 20 miles from their home to purchase binge foods. They were afraid that if they bought items from their local supermarket, their illness might be discovered.

The disorder most commonly develops in the late teens to early twenties and, as with anorexia, a higher percentage of sufferers are female (approximately 90 per cent) although there are still many male sufferers. I spent a number of months at an eating disorders unit during my twenties and one of my fellow patients was a young man who had suffered with bulimia for most of his adult life.

Bulimia can also develop for numerous reasons and is usually associated with a traumatic or challenging event in the sufferer's life. Bulimia can sometimes develop in someone who has originally suffered from anorexia or another eating disorder.

Bulimia sufferers are sometimes unfairly labelled as 'failed anorexics' since they are unable to continually restrict food. From time to time their control breaks, leading to massive binges, which then cause sufferers to find different methods to rid themselves of the calories consumed. This leads them to feel guilty and ashamed of their behaviour which, in turn, causes depression and low self-esteem.

Bulimia can also be an expensive and difficult illness to disguise. It is possible for a sufferer to consume 30,000 calories at a time. That is equivalent to 15 days' food for an average adult. Buying and storing that amount of food can prove difficult, and sufferers can make up elaborate lies to try and cover their tracks. Some sufferers may even shoplift in an attempt to get enough food for their binges.

Although most sufferers believe their bingeing and purging will get rid of all the food they have ingested, this is not the case. The human body actually absorbs the calories in food very quickly. If a sufferer takes large quantities of laxatives, it has been discovered that they actually only dispose of approximately 12 per cent of the food ingested. They may find that their weight has gone down but this is purely because they have passed large quantities of water and dangerously dehydrated their body. As soon as they drink enough to rehydrate themselves, their weight will go back up again.

Similarly, vomiting does not get rid of all the calories eaten. Many calories are actually absorbed by the body and only a percentage of those ingested are removed.

Remembering this point can be helpful for sufferers when they start their recovery. Often, they have accepted all the terrible damage vomiting and purging has inflicted on their bodies because they believed that it got rid of excess calories. When they learn that it actually makes very little difference at all, these behaviours can start to seem quite pointless.

If you feel that you may be suffering from bulimia, try answering the following questions. If you agree with many of them, it is very possible that you have the condition. It is strongly recommended that you seek professional medical advice because of the physically damaging nature of the disorder.

- Do you secretly binge on forbidden foods such as sweets, cakes and biscuits?

- Does guilt cause you to vomit or take laxatives to try and get rid of any food eaten?

- Do you use other dangerous behaviour patterns to rid your body of calories, such as overexercising or fasting?

- Do you find that your jaw and cheeks often look swollen?

- Do you often experience dental problems?

- Do you spend most of your time thinking about food or planning binges?

- Does frequent hunger cause you to crave particular foods?

- Do you suffer from stomach pain and/or constipation?

- Does your throat often feel sore?

- Are your eyes often bloodshot?

- Have you ever vomited blood?

- Do you have chest pains?

- Do you experience painful muscle cramps?

- Do you feel depressed and anxious?

- Do you avoid social situations?

- Do you (or have you ever) used alcohol or drugs to escape from emotional pain?

- Do you visit a number of different shops when you are buying food for a binge? Are you afraid that otherwise people will comment on the amount and type of food that you are purchasing?

- Do you hide food in your house?

- Do you dispose of the wrappers so no one can see how much you have eaten?

- Are you terrified of gaining weight?

- Have you taken slimming pills?

- Do you feel isolated and lonely?

- Is your weight constantly fluctuating?

- Do you feel uncomfortable eating in public places such as restaurants?

- Does food control your life?

Compulsive overeating

This disorder is also known as binge eating disorder. It is a recently recognized condition that has become a growing issue as the quality and quantity of food availability has increased. The disorder leads to obesity, which is now a serious problem throughout the developed world.

Compulsive overeating is similar to bulimia in many ways. Sufferers will consume large volumes of food in a short period of time. They feel out of control and frequently talk of forcing down high-calorie foods without even tasting what they are eating. The major difference with bulimia, though, is that sufferers usually do not purge or vomit afterwards.

Binge eating disorder is still a difficult illness for doctors to diagnose. Everyone overeats from time to time but this alone does not constitute the disorder. The following criteria have to be in place.

- Frequent and regular episodes of eating abnormally large quantities of food (such as consuming more than a day's intake of calories at one sitting).

- Eating faster than normal, often without even tasting the food eaten.

- Eating past the point of feeling full and frequently feeling uncomfortably sick at the end of an episode.

- Eating without feeling in control.

- Eating when there is no feeling of physical hunger.

- Feelings of personal revulsion after a binge.

Although compulsive overeating is still a relatively new condition to be recognized by the medical profession, it is the most common eating disorder. It is also the most prevalent eating disorder among men. There do not seem to be any divisions along ethnic lines and it appears to be a condition which can develop at any time of life (although most frequently in childhood).

Most sufferers are obese, although people of a normal weight can be affected as well. It is estimated that approximately two per cent of the population suffers from compulsive overeating, although the real figure is likely to be far higher.

The causes of the disorder are still not completely clear, although more than 50 per cent of sufferers also have depression. Sufferers often say that they eat in order to cover the emotional pain they are feeling. They state that eating large amounts can block out feelings of loneliness, anger, frustration, sadness, boredom, and any of the inadequacies they may feel in their daily lives.

However, this method of burying pain sends sufferers into a vicious circle of overeating. Every time they feel unhappy, they overeat to compensate. This then leads them to feel disgusted with themselves, which in turn causes them to turn to food again.

Some compulsive overeaters, however, do not binge on large quantities of food at one sitting. Instead, they nibble constantly throughout the day. The key health problem associated with compulsive overeating is obesity and all the medical conditions that accompany the condition.

If you feel that you may suffer from this disorder, try answering the following questions.

- Do you binge on large amounts of food when you are alone?

- Do you eat small or normal-sized meals in company, knowing that you will binge later?

- Do you use food to block out painful thoughts and emotions? Is food a 'comfort' when you feel stressed?

- Do you eat past the point of feeling full?

- Do you frequently feel disgusted with yourself, especially after a binge?

- Do you feel ashamed of your behaviour and keep it a secret?

- Do you try every new diet on the market?

- Do you hate the size and shape of your body?

- Do you avoid exercising?

- Do you feel bad after a binge but do not ever vomit or take laxatives?

- Are you overweight?

- Do you avoid social situations?

- Do you feel depressed but pretend that you are happy?

- Do you dream of being thinner?

- Do you feel angry with yourself for giving in to binges?

If you agree with a number of these questions, it is very possible that you suffer from compulsive overeating and it would be wise to visit a doctor. This is a common condition and professional support and advice can be invaluable in tackling the problem.

Eating disorders not otherwise specified

Eating disorders not otherwise specified (ED-NOS) encompasses all the other disordered eating patterns. The following are some of the more widely recognized problems:

Bulimarexia

As the name suggests, this disorder is a cross between anorexia and bulimia. Sufferers have many of the traits of anorexia – they are underweight and consistently restrict their food intake. They may allow themselves to eat certain low-calorie foods, such as fruit, vegetables, rice cakes, crispbread and yoghurt. However, even after eating this diet food, the guilt is so intense that sufferers force themselves to vomit in a similar way to bulimia sufferers.

Bulimarexia is the most dangerous of all the eating disorders since it combines both fasting and vomiting. When sufferers have a virtually empty stomach and then induce vomiting, they place a tremendous strain on the heart and all the other major organs of the body. They also carry a higher risk of causing a tear in the stomach lining or oesophagus.

Sufferers often feel seriously depressed and even suicidal. They want to have complete control over their diet (in the same way they believe anorexia sufferers do) and feel a failure when they eat and have to resort to vomiting.

Compulsive overexercising (or 'activity disorder')

This disorder concerns physical activity, which is here taken to the extreme. It is more common among men than women and can go hand in hand with body dysmorphia.

Body dysmorphia is an illness in which sufferers believe themselves to be too thin and resort to methods such as bodybuilding. As a result, they can build up their bodies to extreme proportions, and hours of daily exercise can cause sufferers to develop very large muscles.

Exercising is an important part of a healthy life but if it becomes a compulsion it can have dangerous results. Our society promotes the image of toned, lithe bodies as the perfect way to be. Gyms have opened in every town and special membership rates are offered to entice new people to join them.

What starts as a healthy choice can soon develop into an obsession. When a person changes their life around to fit in extra gym sessions, it is likely that there is a problem.

It is recommended that adults engage in three 30-minute sessions of physical exercise per week. Someone who is visiting the gym more than once a day is exercising obsessively.

Exercising can become an addiction because it makes people feel better. Endorphins are released into the brain during exercise and this results in a natural 'high'.

Compulsive overexercisers will not stop or even slow down if they have an injury and this can lead to serious bone and joint problems. Knees and ankles are particularly susceptible to injury.

People who suffer with this disorder are also frequently trying to bury their problems and will go to the gym in order to stop themselves from thinking.

Orthorexia

This is another condition which has only recently been recognized as a problem. Instead of sufferers limiting the amount they eat in general, they focus instead on restricting certain types of food. They will only eat foods that are considered healthy, such as fruit, vegetables, low-fat yoghurts, tofu, seeds, and so on. Cakes, biscuits, sweets or crisps, for example, are not allowed.

Sufferers will have their own obsessive concerns about food and many will avoid foods that contain any fat, preservatives or animal products. The result is that they suffer from malnutrition and can ultimately die from starvation.

Sufferers often have symptoms consistent with obsessive compulsive disorder, as well as with symptoms consistent with anorexia sufferers.

Emetophobia

This is the fear of vomiting or of being around others who are vomiting. It has been listed as the fifth most common phobia by the International Emetophobia Society. This phobia can frequently lead to other disorders, such as agoraphobia, panic attacks, anxiety and depression. In the worst cases, sufferers can become afraid of eating, which sometimes leads to an incorrect diagnosis of anorexia. Emetophobes go to great lengths to avoid being sick. Some sufferers are actually able physically to prevent themselves from ever vomiting by fighting feelings of nausea until they subside.

Pica

This is a disorder in which sufferers will consume non-nutritional substances, such as coal, chalk, paper or soil. It is particularly common in small children and pregnant women. It also appears to be more prevalent in rural and developing countries.

Naturally, eating inedible substances could result in serious health problems, such as lead poisoning, gastrointestinal obstruction, stomach and oesophageal tearing.

Non-specific eating disorders

As well as the illnesses we have identified eating disorders can also be non-specific since they include symptoms from a number of different illnesses. For example:

- a person has all the characteristics of anorexia (starving him- or herself) but is currently overweight

- a person chews his or her food and spits it out instead of swallowing

- a young woman is underweight and is eating very little each day (classic anorexia) and yet she is still having her monthly period.

Disordered eating can take a range of different forms. Do not dismiss a problem just because you do not feel that your particular issues fall into a recognized category.

Body types

There are three main body types and these cannot be changed, no matter how strictly a person diets. An important step in recovery is acknowledging and accepting which body type you have. Look carefully at the descriptions below and identify which category fits your body shape.

Endomorph

People with an endomorphic body type tend to be quite stocky and not particularly tall. Women with this body type have curvy (more generous) figures. Their weight frequently fluctuates and even if they diet regularly they will not achieve a 'skinny' figure.

Ectomorph

At the other end of the scale, people with an ectomorphic body type are tall and slender. They frequently have trouble gaining weight and have smaller breasts, with a boyish figure. Often referred to as 'gamine', this is the typical model look introduced by Twiggy in the 1960s. It would be impossible for an ectomorph to suddenly develop Marilyn Monroe curves since their genetic make-up is too different.

Mesomorph

The mesomorphic body type is generally very muscular. Individuals with this body type are generally taller, with a more angular shape. They seem to stay at a regular weight, although they can both lose or gain pounds quite quickly.

It is vital that eating disorder sufferers accept themselves for who they are. If you are a naturally curvy person then the first step in recovery is accepting this fact. It is always good to have goals to aim for but you should not make these goals impossible. Do not set yourself the task of changing body type – this will only lead to inevitable disappointment and potentially dangerous results.

Exercise 1.1

Body type

Start by identifying your body type. It can help to talk with other family members and identify their body types. You are likely to see a pattern develop. Then write a short statement about what your body type means to you. Has your attitude towards it perhaps led to the development of your eating disorder?

Chapter 2

Choosing Recovery

If you have identified that you have an eating disorder do you also feel that you want to try and make some changes in your life? Living with an eating disorder is both difficult and disruptive but choosing recovery can seem even more terrifying.

In this chapter, we examine the benefits of recovery and show how it can bring huge positive changes into your life. Be realistic though – I have been through recovery myself and it is not always an easy road. As I say to the sufferers who contact me regularly, recovery may sometimes be a difficult process but it is a very worthwhile one.

Before you decide that you want to start recovering, it can be extremely helpful to understand exactly what your eating disorder means to you. In Exercise 2.1 try writing a list of the 'functions' of your eating disorder in your life.

The following is a list of possible 'functions' that you believe the disorder serves and which might help you to compile this list.

- It blocks out traumatic memories.

- It holds your family together.

- It stops you from growing into an adult and taking on more responsibilities.

- It protects you from having adult relationships.

- It allows you to feel in control.

- It helps you to cope with anger by focusing it on yourself.

- It makes you feel different and special.

- It numbs difficult feelings and emotions.

- It causes people to care and look after you.

- It protects you from failing in life because you have an excuse not to try.

- It gives you an identity.

- It allows you to strive for perfection.

- It distracts you from difficult issues in your life.

- It gives you an excuse for social isolation.

Exercise 2.1

Functions of my eating disorder

_____

_____

_____

_____

_____

_____

I hope that this exercise will have helped to show why it feels so difficult to give up your disorder. It is likely that your disorder currently serves a huge number of different roles in your life.

Most eating disorder sufferers feel afraid that if they choose recovery, they will lose too much. For example, some anorexia sufferers fear that their parents will no longer look after them and care for their needs. They will have to face adult responsibilities, find a house, a job, and a partner. All this can appear so daunting that it seems preferable to stay ill. But at what cost?

The dangers of eating disorders
Anorexia
PHYSICAL IMPACT OF ANOREXIA

There are a number of physical problems associated with anorexia which are brought about by the strict starvation diet. These are:

- severe weight loss

- a growth of downy hair ('lanugo') appearing across the body

- decreased pulse and heart rate

- hair loss

- a drop in body temperature which can cause the extremities to turn blue; chilblains may also appear

- diminished or complete loss of sex drive

- dizzy episodes

- weakness and fatigue

- insomnia caused by the body being unable to rest when hungry

- dry and flaky skin

- constipation

- oedema (water retention) causing swelling in the hands and feet

- a sensitivity to light and noise which can make bright lights and loud noises physically painful

- a loss of bone density and possibly osteoporosis (bone thinning)

- anaemia (caused by red and white blood cells not being produced at a fast enough rate).

PSYCHOLOGICAL IMPACT OF ANOREXIA

A range of psychological problems may also develop:

- the sufferer becomes withdrawn and wants to be alone

- a once passive nature can change to an irritable demeanour

- depression is common owing to the lack of nutrients

- lack of concentration – a constant preoccupation with food and weight push all other thoughts aside

- anger at what sufferers see as interference in their illness by doctors or relatives

- a distorted view of their own body develops and sufferers believe that they are 'fat' when they are really very thin.

The human body is extremely resilient and all of these conditions can be reversed if the sufferer begins to eat a full and healthy diet again.

Sadly, a percentage of sufferers do die from their illness. Anorexia nervosa has the highest mortality rate of all mental health conditions. Potentially, as many as 20 per cent of sufferers will lose the battle, either through physical complications from the illness or suicide.

Bulimia
PHYSICAL IMPACT OF BULIMIA

Sufferers of bulimia also experience serious health issues. Many of the physical problems are similar to those of anorexia sufferers. However, there are some additional problems caused by the bingeing and purging.

- Vomiting causes dehydration, which affects the body's electrolyte balance. In particular, potassium becomes deficient and this can affect the heart. A condition called arrhythmia may develop, which can have fatal consequences. For this reason, it is vital for bulimia sufferers to have regular blood tests to determine if their electrolyte levels are healthy.

- Laxatives are also very dangerous medications if overused. They cause the bowel to become 'lazy' so that it will no longer function on its own. This condition is sometimes known as 'cathartic colon'. Taken to excess, it can also lead to serious complications and sufferers have been known to completely lose their bowel.

- Vomiting and laxative abuse will cause sufferers to feel weak and tired. They are likely to have trouble concentrating and their skin may have a green, blotchy appearance.

- A magnesium deficiency (caused by vomiting and purging, or both) can affect the nervous system. Sufferers may see or hear things which are not actually there. They may also tremble and have epileptic fits.

- Some bulimia sufferers are unable to make themselves vomit after eating so they take medications which induce this (emetics). Some of these medicines can seriously damage the heart.

- Teeth can be ruined by constant vomiting since the stomach acid passing the teeth erodes the enamel. If the sufferer also drinks a number of fizzy diet drinks, this can make the problem even worse.

- Vomiting can also cause damage to the stomach and oesophagus. Tears can appear, which can cause the sufferer to vomit blood. It is even possible for bulimia sufferers to die from massive internal bleeding.

- A common problem for bulimia sufferers is delayed stomach emptying. Food remains in the stomach for longer owing to extreme fasting and/or reduced food intake. The whole system slows down and this can leave sufferers feeling bloated and overly full. The speed at which food is processed will return to normal once a regular healthy diet is established.

- Repeated vomiting can also affect the salivary glands, causing them to swell. This leads to a condition known as 'chipmunk cheeks' and can make the sufferer's face appear larger.

- Constant vomiting can also cause acid reflux by loosening the valve that prevents food from leaving the stomach. Stomach acid moves from the stomach and up the oesophagus, resulting in a painful burning sensation.

- Slimming drugs (in the form of appetite suppressants) may be used by bulimia sufferers to try and curb their feelings of hunger and therefore prevent the frequent binges. This may work in the short term, but the pills can cause irritability, anxiety attacks, depression, constipation and even blurred vision.

- Dehydration caused by vomiting and laxative abuse can lead to serious and permanent kidney damage.

- Fatigue is a common side effect of bulimic episodes since the body has not been supplied with enough energy to function properly.

- Headaches can also occur frequently owing to dehydration, stress factors and lack of food.

- Menstrual periods often become irregular or stop altogether. It is important to note that sufferers can still become pregnant. In addition, if birth control pills are being taken, frequent vomiting could mean the sufferer may be unprotected.

- Dramatic weight fluctuations may occur, depending on whether sufferers are in a 'fasting' stage or a 'binge/purge' episode in their cycle.

- It is possible that sufferers will also use other methods of 'escaping', such as excessive use of alcohol or drug abuse.

- Muscle cramps (or tingling in the fingers and around the mouth) may develop due to electrolyte imbalance.

- Vomiting causes the eyes to become red and bloodshot. Eyelids may be swollen and broken blood vessels become visible around the eyes.

- Mouth ulcers and sore throats are common side effects of vomiting.

- Chest pains are also common. The stomach extends behind the ribs and pain in the stomach can be mistaken for chest problems.

- Constipation is a frequent side effect of irregular meals. Often, the diet does not contain enough fibre. Binges frequently focus on high-fat, high-sugar foods, which can be difficult for the bowel to process.

- The metabolic rate can be affected by constant dieting followed by intermittent binges. It prepares for receiving less food by slowing down. A slow metabolism combined with frequent high-calorie binges mean that sufferers can actually gain weight.

- Low blood sugar can also be a side effect of erratic dieting. Known as hypoglycaemia, this condition affects all the major organs, including the brain. It leads to weakness, double vision, sweating, palpitations and feelings of panic.

PSYCHOLOGICAL IMPACT OF BULIMIA

Depression

The disruption to the body chemistry will often trigger depression and mood swings. Sufferers also frequently have low self-esteem since they feel disgusted by their bingeing and purging behaviour. Feelings of sadness may cause the sufferer to withdraw from social activities. A sense of worthlessness and powerlessness can make it hard to perform even simple tasks.

Some sufferers feel so hopeless that they have thoughts of harming themselves or even ending their life. If you are having these thoughts, it is vital that you talk to someone you trust. This could be a friend, relative, colleague or medical professional. If you feel unable to turn to anyone close, always remember that there are crisis helplines that you can telephone. They are listed in the front of telephone directories. See also the Useful Resources at the end of this book.

Depression often goes hand in hand with eating disorders and it will pass as you recover. However, it can be very beneficial to take antidepressants since they can help to motivate sufferers in their recovery.

Anxiety

It might be that sufferers experience anxiety or panic attacks if they are unable to carry out certain behaviours, such as purging after a heavy meal. They may have built up obsessive behaviours and rituals over time, and trying to break these can lead to severe anxiety.

Loss of concentration and memory

Sufferers can become easily distracted and their work may suffer. They may find it difficult to sit through a film or read a book. Their minds are constantly occupied with thoughts of food, weight, calories and body shapes, leaving little time and energy for the rest of their life.

Difficulty making simple decisions

Even trying to choose an outfit for work can be a traumatic experience for many sufferers. These problems can then lead sufferers to feel inadequate and incompetent at day to day living.

Social isolation

Most social events are based around food or have food as a reward. Even a simple trip to the cinema can include chocolate, ice cream, chips or a full meal afterwards as a treat. This can all seem too intimidating for sufferers since they feel unable to use their coping behaviours in public. It is also difficult to socialize when you do not feel at ease with your appearance. It soon becomes easier just to stay home.

Sleep disruption

Bulimia sufferers often experience night disturbances and nightmares caused by chemical imbalances.

All of these physical and psychological problems are a common part of bulimia. As a sufferer, you may have experienced many of them but tried to deny that there was a problem. All of these symptoms are serious and are an indication that you have an illness. Instead of dismissing these symptoms, try instead to use them to motivate yourself into choosing recovery.

Compulsive overeating

The main problem linked to this disorder is obesity. Obesity can cause many other health complications, including diabetes, heart disease, high blood pressure, high cholesterol, arthritis, asthma, gallbladder disease and certain cancers such as bowel or breast cancer (and for women, cancer of the cervix, uterus and ovaries).

Obese adults and children can also experience other problems which can damage their self-esteem and confidence, such as:

- seats on planes, buses or trains may not be large enough for them

- they may be called names – often supposedly affectionately by friends (which can be just as hurtful and degrading)

- inability to compete in sports and other recreational events

- possible prejudice at school or work

- restricted social interaction due to low self-esteem, which can limit opportunities for relationships; this can lead to loneliness and a further drop in confidence

- an inability to perform certain tasks at work, which can result in missed promotional opportunities.

It is important to note that obesity does not cause any more psychological problems in itself than being at an average weight. These issues arise because of a wider prejudice and discrimination that can gradually lower self-esteem.

Our society upholds the concept that 'thin is beautiful', which leaves people who are overweight feeling inadequate and insecure. In other cultures being larger is actually considered to be more desirable since it signifies affluence. In these cultures, the psychological problems of obesity do not exist to the same extent.

Slimming pills

There are many over-the-counter (OTC) medications which claim to help people lose weight quickly. However, there has recently been a great deal of debate as to the safety and effectiveness of these products. It is argued that those which are safe do not seem to aid weight loss at all. The medications which do seem more effective are usually powerful agents which have significant side effects and may be dangerous to health.

Prescription medications

This is a different category of medication and if you feel that you may benefit from these then it is important to talk about this with your doctor. Doctors will prescribe medications at their discretion and may advise you to explore other weight loss methods first. All medications carry possible side effects, though, and it is wise to examine their advantages and disadvantages before starting treatment. Remember, there is no magic cure – losing weight takes time and effort.

Positive effects of recovery

An improvement to both physical and mental health is reason enough for an eating disorder sufferer to choose recovery. However, low self-esteem and an inability to care for themselves can cause some sufferers to dismiss the dangers involved in their illness, as the following extract from my diary shows.

Friday 21 February 1997

I often write things in my diary because there's no one else I can tell. I don't want to bother or upset people with my problems. This is one of those times. I'm too tired at the moment and I'm stressed out with the driving lessons. We went shopping today in Falmouth and I rushed around the shops. I didn't really eat much because I'm not good with meals out and when we got home, I felt dizzy. Then I felt sick and began to shake. This happens quite a lot but it usually passes.

Today though it went on for hours and it was a bit scary. I just put it down to not eating enough. I didn't tell anyone because it would only be making a fuss. I know they talk about heart attacks and anaemia and all that sort of stuff but none of that would ever happen to me. I just needed to pull myself together and stop being so weak.

Here are many of the other positive changes that could occur in your life once you decide on recovery. Look at the list below and then complete Exercise 2.2: write a set of your own positive reasons for choosing recovery. Some reasons might be similar, or even the same, but it is likely that you will have many personal reasons for getting better.

- People will treat you as an equal rather than a child who needs looking after.

- You will be able to make your own choices and decisions.

- You will be able to get a job and earn money so that you can be financially independent.

- You will be able to have a relationship with a partner that could potentially last for a lifetime.

- You will be able to make your own decisions instead of relying on doctors or parents to make them for you.

- You will be able to enjoy social occasions with friends – even having a meal out can, in time, become a treat.

- You will no longer constantly feel afraid about what treatment options will be suggested next, such as inpatient hospital care.

- You will feel physically and mentally healthy.

- You will no longer feel continually hungry, and in response, will stop thinking about food all the time.

- You will avoid doing long-term damage to your body (such as osteoporosis).

- You will no longer be repeatedly affected by triggers.

- You will be able to achieve any dreams you have, from pet ownership to learning how to fly an aircraft.

- You will allow the people who care about you to stop worrying constantly about your health.

- You will gain freedom from the everyday tedium of your eating disorder.

- You will be able to buy and wear new clothes.

- You will lose your disordered identity and instead discover your real personality.

- Your free time will be available for you to have fun – it will no longer be tied up with eating disorder obsessions.

- You will be able to make long-term plans.

- Most important of all, you will feel happier.

Exercise 2.2

Positive effects of my recovery

_____

_____

_____

_____

_____

_____

When you have completed Exercise 2.2, examine it carefully. All the items you have listed are motivational statements which can help you through some of the more difficult parts of your recovery. It is important to have goals to aim at and these are all positive goals.

Do one of the following.

- Make a large poster listing all your reasons for recovery. This can then be placed somewhere important so that you can re-read these statements when you are feeling low.

- Make up some cards with one of your positive statements on each one. These can then be carried around with you and used as motivational tools during your recovery.

Exercise 2.3

Visualization

- Try to imagine your life without the eating disorder.

- Is it really something that you want to live with for the rest of your life?

What would you be doing right now if your disorder was not holding you back?

Reasons why you might not want to recover

It is, of course, likely that you have many reasons why you feel it is not to your advantage to recover. This is natural since recovery can be a difficult process and sufferers often feel intimidated and insecure about attempting it. It can feel as though they have too much to lose by surrendering their disorder.

On closer examination, though, many of these reasons are actually disadvantages, which are holding you back. When I listed my own reasons for holding on to my illness, one of the points was as follows.

> People will comment on how I look and make remarks such as
> 'You look so much healthier now.'

I was concerned that this would be a comment on my new size and an indication of my weight gain rather than a compliment. Most people view compliments such as these as one of life's joys – they certainly would not see it as a reason to remain ill.

The following are some of my other reasons for staying anorexic. After each statement, I have examined whether it is actually a good reason for holding on to an eating disorder.

> I don't have to take risks and so I can't fail.

Taking risks is all part of life. Some will turn out well, whereas others may not pay off, but all of them help you to gain experience. Spending time with someone new is a risk – you might not get on and you could spend a couple of awkward hours together.

However, there is an equal chance that you could really like this person and he or she might become a good friend who may even help you with your recovery. By avoiding risks, you can miss out on many of the joys of life.

> People won't care for me as much – they only pay me attention
> because I'm not well.

If people care about you then this will always remain true. They would not have to spend so much time worrying about you if you have recovered. This means that you can spend more enjoyable quality time together. If you are, unfortunately, in any kind of relationship where the other person does not show care, then forcing yourself to be ill will not change his or her attitude.

> If I recovered, I might encounter problems which will make me
> feel inadequate.

By developing an eating disorder, many sufferers 'step out' of everyday life. Normal problems no longer concern them as they focus on food-related issues instead. When you start recovering, you will begin to take on new responsibilities and so will encounter problems that may initially feel difficult to tackle.

This is just part of a healthy life. Everyone experiences daily problems and also makes mistakes from time to time. Instead of retreating and allowing yourself to feel inadequate, try to learn from these mistakes. Talk to those around you and work out how to tackle the problem better in the future.

> Eating properly makes me feel anxious, guilty and uncomfortable.

It is true that recovery may not always be an easy process. During your illness, you have trained your mind to reject food in the belief that it is the enemy. Now it is time to re-educate your mind. This process will take time and may cause you to experience some difficult emotions but this is temporary.

Each time you sit with the guilt after eating (instead of using your disordered behaviours to make yourself feel better) you are one step closer to recovery. Every battle will lessen the hold the disorder has over you until, one day, the feelings of guilt will evaporate.

> My periods will restart and my body will develop into that of an adult female.

Many anorexia sufferers feel relief when their periods stop and they can revert to a child-like state. However, this is neither mentally nor physically healthy. Physical damage will begin to occur as soon as periods stop. A lack of oestrogen can lead to bone-thinning and osteoporosis developing in later life.

It is also not psychologically healthy for an adult woman to have the body of a child. As an adult, you can choose if you want to have a partner and relationships – no one can force this upon you. And you certainly do not need to make yourself seriously ill to hide from it. If this is true for you, it could help to talk over your relationship fears and worries with a doctor or therapist.

> I will experience feelings and hunger, and respond to them in a normal way.

This is a sign that your body is healing. When you have suffered with an eating disorder for a number of months or years, you may no longer recognize when your body is actually feeling hunger. It is likely that the normal signals will have become distorted until eventually you have trained yourself to ignore genuine hunger pangs.

When you begin to eat normally again, you will initially feel overly full but quite quickly your body will adapt and it will start to feel hunger a few hours after eating. This is a healthy sign which shows you are making progress. It does not mean that you will suddenly begin eating uncontrollably.

> I am worried that it will feel hurtful and frightening if not everyone is happy when I am recovering.

It is normal for everyone to have a few people in their life who do not always wish them well. Pride, competitive natures and insecurity lead some people to hope that their friends or relatives do not achieve more than them. It may be unsettling to think that there could be some close to you who are content with you staying ill.

However, it is possible that by staying in the 'sick role', you make them feel better about their own life. It may be that your low self- esteem caused you to try to please them all the time. As you recover, you will become more assertive and successful and they may find this difficult to manage. It is important to choose to continue with your recovery and distance yourself from any people who are a negative influence on your life.

> I do not want to go through periods of 'feeling fat'.

This will not actually be a new feeling since most sufferers say that even at their lowest weight, they felt 'fat'. Learn to accept that feelings are *not* fact. They are often illogical impulses generated by the negative thoughts that you are having about yourself.

The above were my major reasons for wanting to remain ill. I eventually realized that the list of positive reasons for recovery clearly outnumbered the reasons for keeping hold of the disorder. I also realized that each argument for staying ill was very easily disputed.

Now, go back and look at the list you made earlier of the functions of your eating disorder in Exercise 2.1. Take each statement you made and examine it from every angle. Is this really a valid reason to remain ill? Remember everything that you are giving up just so that you can retain a disorder that is controlling (and destroying) your life.

Try writing a counterargument for each statement that you have written. It can help to imagine that a friend is telling you their reasons for keeping ill. Would you encourage them in their disorder or would you show them the positive aspects of regaining their lives? As you work through this list, you will discover that it is actually quite difficult (if not impossible) to find a genuine reason for keeping hold of your illness.

It is important that your recovery is not conditional on any event in your life. Sufferers will frequently play games with the idea of recovery, telling themselves that when a certain event happens they will then begin recovery.

Anorexia sufferers often make plans dependent upon their weight. I know that this was certainly true in my own case, and I would tell myself that when I reached a specific weight then I would start recovery. However, this was just an excuse since I was always changing this target weight.

When I did eventually choose recovery, it was not based on any single event – it was because I realized how the disorder was holding me back and ruining my life. If your plans for recovery are conditional it is likely that you will also keep finding another reason to avoid it.

I would like to end this chapter with one final positive comment. Sufferers often ask me if recovery is even possible. From my own experience, I can say without any doubt that it is. I am also regularly contacted by many former sufferers who are thrilled to be able to say that they have now fully recovered.

Chapter 3

Letting Go of Your Illness

From my own experiences, and those of the people who contact me, it would be fair to say that eating disorders can be long-term illnesses. Most sufferers have had their disorder for many months or years before they look seriously at the idea of recovery. Even then, it is often someone else or some event which has pushed them in this direction.

Eating disorders can become sufferers' entire identity and they are afraid that if they give up their illness, they will be left as simply an empty shell. I felt certain that this was going to be true for me, although it turned out to be just one of the many myths which surround recovery.

When I mentioned my concerns to a therapist, I was told that as I gradually gave up the anorexia (together with all of its associated thoughts and rituals) I would free up lots of time. This time would then become filled with work, hobbies and new relationships which would help me to grow and develop as a person. This proved to be true and, looking back now, I cannot believe that I had enough time for the eating disorder.

The myth that your eating disorder is your identity may be one of the reasons why you might feel unable to surrender your illness. In this chapter, we are going to look at the reasons why people try to hold on to their illness rather than choosing recovery.

Eating disorders fit into an unusual category in terms of treatment. In most situations, when you have an illness, you will visit your local doctor in the hope that he or she will be able to cure you.

However, many eating disorder sufferers are frightened by the idea of recovery. They see their eating disorder as a friend rather than a medical condition (another myth) and think that letting go of it would be impossible. They often avoid seeing a doctor and only attend when they are forced to by someone close or because of a dramatic situation (such as fainting at school or at work).

Recovery timetable

The length of time that you have been ill with your eating disorder can be linked to how long it will take you to recover. Doctors generally believe that an eating disorder sufferer will require a month of recovery for every year that he or she has been ill. So, for example, I had anorexia for 14 years and my recovery was therefore expected to take approximately 14 months. This was a good projection and I was eating normally without eating-disordered thoughts within 18 months of my recovery starting.

It can often help sufferers to accept that recovery is a slow process as this feels less intimidating. Most sufferers fear that they will be expected to make large changes overnight and this is not the case. A slow recovery is more likely to be a permanent one.

Drawing up a plan can often help sufferers to design their recovery at a speed they can manage. Work out exactly what changes you would like to make each month and then record how close you came to reaching your goals. Table 3.1 illustrates this.

Table 3.1 A design for recovery

	Projected recovery	Actual recovery
Month 1	Increase calories by 100 each week	Managed to increase diet by 75 calories each week
	Cut down on exercise by 10 minutes per day	Cut down on exercise by 7 minutes per day
Month 2	Stop taking laxatives and increase soluble fibre	Stopped taking all laxatives with doctor's help
Month 3	Cut down to weighing myself only once a day	Cut down to weighing myself only once a day
	Join a support group	Found out details about group; perhaps join next month

Exercise 3.1

Mythbusters

The following are some more commonly held myths about eating disorders which sufferers often accept as fact. Look at each one in turn. Have you ever held any of these beliefs?

Before you look at the truth (listed below each myth) try filling out your own response in the gaps provided. Do not respond as an eating disorder sufferer. Imagine instead that you have no problems with food or body issues.

Myth 1

If I choose to recover and ask for help, I will be forced to eat huge amounts of food.

Your response

_____

_____

_____

Truth

If you choose to ask for help then you are taking control of your eating disorder voluntarily. If you need to go to hospital, doctors and nurses will consult with you and together you can draw up a treatment plan that you feel comfortable with.

Myth 2

My eating disorder makes me more popular.

Your response

_____

_____

_____

Truth

It may be that people are currently paying attention to you because you are ill. However, it is impossible for them to have a normal relationship with you this way. They may be worried about upsetting you and concerned about your health so that they take on the role of a carer. If you were recovered then you could enjoy normal events with other people, such as shopping or a meal out.

Myth 3

People will stop caring for me if I am well.

Your response

_____

_____

_____

Truth

If people love you then they will always care about you. If you were well then it would be less frightening for them and you would see that they cared for you even when you were safe. Think how you would feel if someone you loved were seriously ill. I am sure that you would feel deeply concerned and under a great deal of stress. Do you want all the people you care about, and who care about you, to feel that uncomfortable?

Myth 4 (for anorexia sufferers)

Once I start eating, I won't be able to stop.

Your response:

_____

_____

_____

Truth

Recovery from anorexia does not actually work like this. When you are restricting your intake you will be starving hungry and thinking of nothing but food. It feels as though you could eat forever. However, when you begin to have regular meals, your body no longer constantly craves food. You find that you eat what is on your food plan and then naturally feel full. When your body has regular food, your blood sugar level becomes stable and you can eat a normal amount without wanting more.

Myth 5

My eating disorder allows me to feel in control.

Your response

_____

_____

_____

Truth

Once you develop an eating disorder, you actually lose all control over your eating and then, ultimately, your life. The eating disorder firmly takes charge and it is then in control of your actions. If you really believe that your illness allows you control over food then why does it stop you from eating what you want?

Myth 6

The eating disorder in my head is telling me the truth and everyone else is just being kind or trying to interfere.

Your response

_____

_____

_____

Truth

Your illness lies to you all the time and that is the way it exerts control. It tells you that food is bad when the truth is that food is an essential part of life. You will also find that, in general, people are not kind just for the sake of it. If they say that you are a nice person then try to believe them rather than the poisonous lies which the eating disorder tells you.

Myth 7

If I lose control of my diet, I will balloon in size.

Your response

_____

_____

_____

Truth

It is a fact that people need to eat an extra 3500 calories on top of their normal intake just to gain a single pound. This means that it is impossible to balloon in size. Gaining weight is a slow process and it takes a lot of food in order to make it happen.

Myth 8

My eating disorder stops me from dealing with or thinking about my other problems.

Your response

_____

_____

_____

Truth

It is true that an eating disorder can prevent you from thinking about anything other than food or weight. However, this is not a healthy or sustainable situation and if you have a problem in your life, you will eventually need to face it. Ask for help and try to work out solutions to your concerns. Developing an eating disorder only causes additional serious (and potentially life-threatening) problems.

Myth 9

No one else understands what it is like to have an eating disorder.

Your response

_____

_____

_____

Truth

Many people have suffered from eating disorders and, as a result, it is becoming an illness which is more widely understood. It is important to give people a chance to offer you support. Try to explain to them just how you are feeling and also let them know how best they can help. You may feel less alone as you read this book so perhaps share any parts which you feel best describe your particular situation with friends, family or therapists.

Myth 10

Men are only attracted to thin women.

Your response

_____

_____

_____

Truth

If you take the time to look at which magazines men enjoy reading, you will find that the models in them are curvy and have well-developed bodies. Whenever polls are taken, the majority of men prefer women who 'have a bit of meat on their bones'. It is very rare for men to express a preference for thin women, who are often thought of as having 'boyish' figures (with no bust or hips) and are viewed as less attractive.

Myth 11

I am ashamed of my eating-disordered behaviours.

Your response

_____

_____

_____

Truth

Feeling ashamed of eating-disordered behaviour is common among sufferers but it is an unnecessary feeling. If you are talking with a doctor, he or she is likely to have heard numerous similar stories (and many that are more extreme) and should remain non-judgemental.

It may be harder for you to tell friends or family members since you might worry about their reaction. I cannot guarantee that you will always receive a positive response from loved ones – sometimes fear for your safety can cause them to become upset. However, I do know that recovery comes about when you are open and honest about your problems. Eating disorders are illnesses like any other and sufferers should not feel ashamed to discuss them.

Myth 12

People who interfere just want to make me fat.

Your response

_____

_____

_____

Truth

It is important to understand that no one wants to make you 'fat'. Recovery is about reaching a healthy weight for your height, and doctors simply want you to be healthy.

Myth 13

I do not deserve food – I need to punish myself.

Your response

_____

_____

_____

Truth

Everyone deserves food – it is a basic human right. Often, sufferers feel that they need to punish themselves due to low levels of self-esteem and self-confidence. Guilt at having eaten a meal used to leave me feeling as though I needed to self-harm. This is just a part of the illness, however, and, regardless of how powerful it may seem at the time, it is only a feeling. It is _not_ the truth.

Myth 14

My eating disorder allows me to show how unhappy I am.

Your response

_____

_____

_____

Truth

Eating disorders are often used as a way of physically expressing internal pain that the sufferer feels unable to share verbally. It is important to learn how to talk about your painful emotions with your loved ones. We should all be able to communicate difficult feelings in a calm and safe way. If you feel unable to speak about your concerns, writing down your thoughts instead is an equally good way of letting those around you know about your problems.

Myth 15

I am proud of myself when I manage to control my hunger.

Your response

_____

_____

_____

Truth

There are many things to be proud of in life but it is not an achievement to make yourself seriously ill. Hunger is a vital signal from your body that it requires food and this should not be ignored.

These 15 myths are all common reasons that sufferers give for not attempting recovery. The idea of letting go of your disorder may seem very daunting but stop and look at all of the things that it is currently preventing you from doing.

The following exercises may help you to see just how restrictive an eating disorder can be.

Exercise 3.2

Positives and negatives

List all of the good and bad points about your eating disorder in two separate columns. When you have completed this exercise, you may well find that a lot of the points you have listed as positive are actually negatives in disguise. When I did this exercise, for example, I listed 'losing weight' as a positive in favour of keeping hold of my eating disorder. However this was in reality a negative since losing weight had led to my becoming seriously physically ill and extremely unhappy.

Exercise 3.3

List what you are missing

Try writing down the things that you will be able to do if you choose to beat your eating disorder. In my own case, I had to give up work because I was too physically weak and so this was one of my major reasons for recovery.

When you start recovering, it can help to keep this list to hand. If you are having a bad day, looking back at the list can help to motivate you and remind you exactly what you are working towards.

Another reason that many sufferers feel unable to let go of their illness is a fear of joining the adult world. This is especially true of anorexia sufferers, where the illness actually causes a regression in development. Female sufferers find that their periods stop and that they revert to a state where they need to be looked after by their parents once more. Fear of issues like getting a job, having a relationship or owning property can be so intimidating for some that it can leave them too afraid to embark on a healthy life.

Miranda, for example, was a 'straight A' student and, at age 18, she left home for university. Before she reached her nineteenth birthday though, she was already in hospital being treated for severe anorexia. After two months in hospital, she spent six months back at home recovering. At the age of 20, she returned to university again to begin her second year. She spent her twenty-first birthday in hospital being fed through a naso-gastric tube. This time though she was in a psychiatric hospital and therapy was given to her every day.

Gradually, Miranda came to accept that she was terrified of failing in the adult world. She realized that if she did not complete her degree, she would not be able to get the type of job that she was expected to have. Her anorexia prevented her from finishing the degree and therefore she could remain a child and keep living at home with her parents. Slowly, she was helped to accept that her fear of adult responsibilities should not hold her back from pursuing her goals.

Try to identify your fears (see Exercise 3.4). Now look back carefully at each point. Are these fears preventing you from moving on with your life? Are you allowing your fears to control you and cause you to hold on to a potentially life-threatening illness?

Whether you have one fear on your list or a whole page, it is likely that they will seem very daunting to you and might even appear impossible to tackle. It is unrealistic to expect you to suddenly change overnight and banish all your fears. However, I do know from personal experience that when you do face your fears, they are never as intimidating as you imagine.

My father-in-law had a very helpful phrase – 'Nothing is ever as good or as bad as you imagine.' It is easy to build up fears in your head until it feels as though it is impossible to beat them. Every fear can be conquered, and if you can face them, you will become a much stronger person.

Our fears are based around the belief that we will not be able to cope with a particular situation. When you actually face one of these potentially terrifying situations, you generally find that you can cope and often handle the situation extremely well. If you continue to use this workbook and complete all of the relevant exercises, you will find that you automatically confront many of your fears. As you face them, you will begin to make some real progress towards recovering.

Exercise 3.4

Write down your fears

My fears

Try making a list of your fears. Is there anything which is causing you to hang on to your eating disorder? Are you afraid of change? Fearful of getting a job? Unsure about living on your own? Even if the fears feel irrelevant to your eating disorder, list them all here

Exercise 3.5

Positive influences

When you are considering recovery, it is important to surround yourself with positive influences. Unfortunately, you may find that not all of the people in your life are supportive and helpful. It may even be beneficial to some people for you to remain ill.

Draw a diagram with yourself in the centre and all the other key people in your life around the outside. Now link yourself to these people with either a positive (blue) line or a negative (red) line. This can help you to see more clearly who is an aid to your recovery and who could hinder it. Try to keep contact with your negative influences as

Exercise 3.6

Recognizing your hunger

It can be difficult for eating disorder sufferers to admit that they feel hungry. They often believe that if they do acknowledge it then people will force them to eat. This exercise does not expect sufferers to act on feelings of hunger but just to record them honestly when they occur. This will allow them to start getting more in touch with their body and its needs.

Write down whenever you feel hungry over the course of a week and give a rating out of ten for each entry (with '1' being slightly peckish and '10' being starving hungry). When you have compiled this week's list, you are likely to be able to see a pattern. We all get hungry at times but it is unhealthy to feel ravenous – aim to add an extra snack into your diet when you are feeling this way.

Exercise 3.7

Write a letter to your disorder

There is one final exercise with which I would like to end this chapter. The idea of letting go of your eating disorder is quite a monumental decision for most sufferers. It can help to actually say goodbye to the illness.

Many sufferers have let me know that they found it very beneficial to write a farewell letter to their disorder. This letter can take any form you like. You can talk about the pain it has caused you or the difficulty you have had in letting go of it. You may even feel that there are some good memories that you want to include.

Ultimately, though, this letter is to say goodbye. It is time to separate yourself from the illness that has controlled your life for so long. You are no longer going to believe that your eating disorder is a part of you. It is not your best friend – you are now two separate entities and you are going to fight it until it disappears completely.

Chapter 4

Coping with Guilt

Probably the most common question I get asked is 'How do you deal with the feelings of guilt after you've eaten?' This was also a question that I frequently asked my therapists. Often it is these intense feelings of guilt which sufferers experience that prevent them from beginning recovery.

Unfortunately there is no simple answer to this question, although this chapter is intended to help sufferers accept these feelings of guilt as just a sign that they have chosen the healthy path to recovery.

When sufferers develop their disorder, they begin to programme their mind into believing that food is bad. Whenever they feel hungry, they tell themselves that they are behaving badly and that they need to deny themselves nourishment in order to be good people.

If this continues for months, or even years, it becomes a regular pattern of behaviour. It no longer feels normal to eat food as a natural response to hunger since this now feels wrong. This means that when they do finally eat, they are overwhelmed by intense feelings of guilt. Reprogramming your mind to accept food as healthy, natural and enjoyable is key to recovery.

Sufferers often feel particularly guilty about eating any extra food since they imagine that a single square of chocolate will cause them to balloon in size. However, it can be helpful to bear in mind that it takes 3500 calories (in addition to a normal day's intake) to put on just one pound.

Three and a half thousand calories is equal to 55 slices of bread, 17.5 chocolate éclairs, 70 apples or 650g (1.5lb) of chocolate. This equation shows that one small piece of chocolate will not suddenly increase your weight. Gaining weight (or losing it, in the case of compulsive overeaters) is a slow process which needs to take place at a steady pace.

I received a great deal of therapy aimed at encouraging me to deal with guilt and I found that two of these concepts were particularly helpful.

- **Feelings are *not* facts**. Just because you feel guilty, it does not mean that you have actually done anything wrong. Food is a basic human need to which we are all entitled. It can help to make up some cards or even posters containing phrases such as 'Food is vital for my health', 'I need to eat' and 'It is *not* wrong to eat food'. Put these cards or posters in prominent places and look at them when you are feeling food-related guilt. Repetition is a vital part of therapy. Re-reading positive messages or affirmations may seem tedious at times but when you consider how often you voluntarily repeat negative thoughts, it may take a little while before you can turn the tide.

- **Certain feelings are a part of recovery**. A therapist once said to me, 'Accept you feel rotten but don't let it affect your resolve to recover.' If you can accept the feelings and just continue to eat anyway, they will pass in time. It will not be an instant process but each time you are able to cope with the guilt and carry on, the entire process will get a little easier.

There are other events which are also difficult for eating disorder sufferers because of guilt, and food shopping, in particular, may be a challenge for various different reasons.

Grocery shopping

Anorexia sufferers often find it hard to put food in their basket which contains an 'unsafe' number of calories. I would often attempt to place higher-calorie foods in my basket at the supermarket but these would feel too uncomfortable and, a few minutes later, I would abandon them in another aisle. I would find that by the end of a shopping trip, I had once again bought only what I felt were 'safe' foods.

Bulimia sufferers and compulsive overeaters often go shopping with the idea that they will binge on their purchases as soon as they get home. It is important to break these patterns of behaviour, and the following are methods that can help.

- Never go to a food store when you are hungry. Typical binge foods, such as cakes, biscuits and chocolate, will seem almost irresistible if you are feeling empty.

- Make a list in advance of the food you will need for your plan and work from this instead. A new chocolate bar or special offer on cakes might be very tempting when you are in the store but if it is not on the list then it should not be purchased.

- Having lots of food in the house might be tempting in the early stages of recovery. Be honest with yourself, though. Does having a week's shopping in the larder encourage you to binge? If this is the case, consider shopping more frequently for smaller amounts of food. If you need to go shopping on a daily basis, buy only what you need to maintain your food plan for the day.

- Consider asking a friend or relative to go shopping with you. Do not hand over responsibility to him or her, however. It is important that you are able to shop sensibly yourself. We all need support during traumatic events and a friendly chat while shopping could help to alleviate the tension.

- Plan an activity for when you return home after shopping. Many bulimia sufferers or compulsive overeaters will binge as soon as they return from the supermarket. Make sure that you have company or an activity to do so that you can help avoid this danger period. Urges do fade given time. It may be that you currently feel that if you experience an urge to binge, you always have to give in to this feeling. Fight the urge by distracting yourself and gradually this impulse will peak and begin to fade.

- Start to include foods which you view as 'unsafe' in your daily eating plan so that you can accept that you are allowed to enjoy them. The aim is to reach a point of 'normal eating' without bingeing and vomiting. For this to happen, it is important to eat from all of the different food groups without any restricted items.

Draw up a daily eating plan

As mentioned earlier in this chapter, eating often engenders feelings of guilt in sufferers. A set eating plan is one way of dealing with the constant debates that they have with themselves on a daily basis. With a set plan, the sufferer does not have to make difficult choices throughout the day since these are now pre-planned.

Often, guilt arises because sufferers feel that they have made the wrong decision on the spur of the moment. With a fixed diet, this is eliminated. The element of choice is removed and they simply have to follow through with the planned menus instead.

Before you begin this exercise, try to remember that your aim is to eat normally. For women, this means consuming between 1800 and 2200 calories per day and, for men, between 2200 and 2800 calories each day.

If you are eating less than this amount, you are restricting your diet in some way. You may be eating smaller portions than are normal or you might be eating only diet products. If you are eating less than you need on a daily basis then your body will be losing weight and your illness will continue to progress.

If you are eating more than the recommended amount then it is likely that you are either consuming large portions at each meal or you are bingeing on high-calorie comfort foods between meals. Neither of these patterns is healthy and if you have recognized your own pattern of disordered eating then you need to make some changes.

Often, eating disorder sufferers think of themselves as simply 'dieting'. They are always looking for ways to cut calories from their daily intake. If you are to eat normally, you will again need to train your mind to think like a non-dieter. People who do not diet rely on their body to tell them when to eat and how much. They gauge how much to eat by judging how full they are feeling.

For eating disorder sufferers, the feelings of hunger and fullness are difficult to cope with. Anorexia sufferers will frequently even deny having any feelings of hunger at all. Eventually, they can reach the point of being uncertain what spontaneous hunger actually feels like.

Bulimia sufferers and compulsive overeaters tend to ignore the feeling of fullness and continue eating. They will often continue to the point of feeling physically sick and unwell. When they are hungry, they may feel that bingeing and vomiting are their only options. However, when a sufferer returns to a normal healthy diet, the desire to binge will begin to subside.

The long-term goal is to be able to eat according to your own body's signals. This will not be possible in the early stages of recovery since eating disorders affect the way that the body reacts. In the short term, sufferers need to rely instead on a set eating plan. Each day, you will have to eat your meals and snacks at the same time so that you can retrain your body into accepting food at regular intervals.

If you are going to follow a set eating plan then you will need to be strict. Everything on the plan must be eaten each day regardless of how you are feeling or what you are thinking. Following this plan will prevent you from restricting or overeating.

The plan is broken down into three meals (breakfast, lunch and dinner) and three snacks (mid-morning, mid-afternoon and before sleep) each day. The idea of a plan may seem very intimidating at first but remember that you can build your diet slowly. No one will expect an anorexia sufferer to go from maintaining a very limited diet each day to a complete eating plan overnight. Your plan will reflect the different stages in your recovery and food can be added at different intervals so that progress is continually being made.

You will need to put aside a little time each day to work out the following day's menu. Alternatively, you may want to work a week in advance by setting aside time during the weekend to construct a seven-day plan.

Remember that this will only be necessary for the length of time that you are recovering. You will not need to write out food plans for the rest of your life. This is just a short-term recovery aid.

It may be that you currently have a nutritionist or therapist who can help you to design a healthy eating plan especially suited to your needs. If you are going to work out your own menu, try turning to the recipe section of this book. The guidelines and recipes will help you to organize a suitable eating plan containing the required number of calories for recovery to begin.

Distraction techniques

When sufferers begin a new diet plan, they are likely to experience renewed feelings of guilt when eating. Distraction techniques can be a useful therapeutic tool during difficult times at the end of meals.

It is vital to break the cycle of destructive behaviour and if you can manage this just once, then you can do it again. Each time you break the rules of your eating disorder, you are one step closer to full recovery.

Exercise 4.1

Distracting yourself

If you know in advance that you are likely to feel guilty after a meal, try preparing yourself in advance. When the guilt begins, *do not* resort to negative behaviour such as bingeing, purging, overexercising or self-harming.

Instead, do something positive that you know will make you feel better. This can be anything from putting on a CD or reading a book to trying a new creative hobby. Redirect all the negative energy and fear that you are currently experiencing into something constructive.

Remember to take action as soon as the meal has ended because, if you delay, your resolve to stay strong may weaken. Save special treats such as watching your favourite film or TV show for the times when you are likely to feel bad.

I know from my own recovery that this is not always an easy task. Guilt is a powerful emotion but it can be beaten. I am now able to eat any food I choose without counting calories or feeling guilt which is something I never expected to be able to achieve.

Exercise 4.2

Stop negative behaviour

It may be that you use negative behaviour to cope with your guilt. If this is the case, try making it more difficult for yourself to carry out these tasks.

If you are overexercising or vomiting, for example, arrange to be with someone at the time you would normally be tempted to do this. If you take laxatives, buy a small lockable box and put the key in an inaccessible place. This will give you the time to recognize just what you are doing and allow you to stop before making the unhealthy choice.

Exercise 4.3

Role reversal

This exercise concerns role reversal. Often, when people suffer from a disorder, they do not realize how badly they are behaving towards themselves. They would never behave in such a cruel and thoughtless manner to anyone else they knew so why treat themselves so differently?

In this exercise you learn how to look after yourself in the same way that you would look after a friend. Whenever you have a problem, try writing this down and outlining your behaviour in response to it. Then try to look objectively at the issue and respond as you would if it were your friend's problem.

For example:

Problem:

You feel guilty after eating a meal.

Your response:

I ended up crying and calling myself names. I want to hurt myself for being so bad.

A friend's response:

This person needs a hug. She has been very brave and has eaten food that will help her to recover. I want her to give herself some praise and have a treat for her achievement.

Now try taking some of the issues that you are struggling with and reverse the situation. Remember that it is not yourself who you are treating badly – it is a friend. Do you really want to hurt your friend?

Problem:

_____

Your response:

_____

_____

A friend's response:

_____

_____

Problem:

_____

Your response:

_____

_____

A friend's response:

_____

_____

Pushing the boundaries

Now that you have some methods of coping with the guilt, you may feel it is time to begin challenging yourself. There will be many eating-disordered behaviours which feel impossible to break and so these are the ones which are now important to tackle.

The following activity helps to confront two of the most difficult issues.

Try eating a food which contains an unknown number of calories. When I suffered from anorexia, I knew the calorific value of every morsel of food that I put in my mouth. However, this is not a healthy way to live since it is limiting as well as being highly obsessional.

To tackle this activity it can help to have the support of a friend, relative or therapist. There are two possible ways to approach this activity.

- When you are shopping, pick up a product which you do not usually buy. Put it in your basket but at no point can you look at the nutritional information on the label.

- Go to a café alone (or with a supportive friend) and choose an item off the menu which you have never ordered before. Try and avoid foods

that have no calories, such as a green salad. If you do select a salad,
make sure that it comes with protein-rich food such as cheese.

Both of these approaches should be repeated as regularly as possible. They will stretch your boundaries and help to expand your safety zone. Your months or years as an eating disorder sufferer are likely to have increasingly limited your diet. Now is the time to widen it again.

One final point about these two activities is that each time you use them, make sure you keep trying new foods. Use the distraction techniques learnt earlier in this chapter to help cope with feelings of guilt. Also, do remember to reward yourself each time you succeed at any of these tasks.

Chapter 5

Writing a Thoughts and Feelings Diary

Sufferers often use their disorders to bury any difficult or painful emotions which they are experiencing. It can therefore be very beneficial to start writing these thoughts and feelings down in a diary. For recovery to take place, it is necessary to accept these emotions and learn how to cope with them on a daily basis.

Eating disorders are frequently thought of as shameful illnesses by sufferers. They hate many of the associated behaviours such as restricting, overexercising, vomiting and purging. As a result, they may even pretend that these actions are not actually happening.

Writing about the thoughts and feelings behind these behaviours can help them to understand why they are acting this way. This can then lead them to discover new and positive ways of reacting to similar situations in the future.

In time, they may also feel able to share their writings with doctors, therapists, friends and family. This can show them more clearly the problems the sufferer is experiencing and teach them how they can best help with recovery.

At certain points during my own illness, I felt unable to verbalize the pain that I was feeling. If a therapist asked me how I was coping, I would immediately reply that I was 'fine'. I felt that I was a nuisance to medical staff and that I took up too much of their time.

Once I began writing my diary though, I took this with me to every medical appointment and I was able to show them how I was really feeling through my writing. In turn, they could then tailor their treatment to meet my needs.

There really is only one rule when writing a thoughts and feelings diary, and that is to be honest. This diary is to help you express your true feelings and there is no point in lying to yourself.

It will not be easy to always record the truth – you might not like how you may have behaved towards someone, for example. It is only possible to learn about yourself through honesty, though. It is important to accept that we all make mistakes in life but they are not wasted opportunities if you can learn from them.

You may find that writing in your diary leaves you feeling very emotional at times. This is no bad thing, however. It was obvious through my diary entries that I understood a great deal about my family dynamics and was also able to talk about the abuse that I suffered.

Diary extracts

The following are some extracts from my diaries, to give an idea of how they helped me to understand more about myself and my illness.

A thoughts and feelings diary can be very helpful in recording how you are feeling during therapy exercises.

Tuesday 27 August 1997

I actually did it. I ate something off my list of 'impossible' foods. I chose a packet of ready-made sandwiches. It took me a long time to choose because I had to look at how many calories there were in each pack.

I wish that I could have just picked out the flavour that I most fancied eating without considering the calorie content. Maybe that will come in time. I guess at least I made some progress today.

I also didn't pick the lowest calorie option. The one I chose was sort of in the middle of the range.

It was a difficult morning as I felt scared about eating them from the moment I picked them out. I did manage to eat them all, which is the first step.

I am struggling with feelings of guilt and self-hatred now but that's OK.

Your diary can teach you a lot about yourself, which may be surprising. For example, many people dismiss dreams as irrelevant but they can contain a great deal of information about your mental and physical health.

During my anorexic years, I had constant nightmares. Physically, my body was hungry all of the time and this led to my continually experiencing disturbing dreams. Mentally, I was trying to accept that a number of people had abused me throughout my life, leaving my levels of confidence and self-esteem extremely low.

Wednesday 20 August 1997

I am very tired tonight as I'm having so many nightmares. One I had last night really stuck in my head because I felt scared of the way I behaved.

Someone hurt me (which I could accept) but they also hurt someone I loved (which I couldn't bear) and I really started shouting at them.

These feelings of anger frightened me. I don't want to even write about them here because that's admitting they exist. I don't want to have feelings like that inside me.

Your diary can also show how you feel about your family. We are led to believe that all families get along smoothly and that they will always pull together in a crisis. This is an idea which is constantly reinforced in books, films and on television shows.

However, it is within the family that problems often begin. Even from an early age, siblings frequently have a rivalry with one another and feel angry or disappointed if their brother or sister is more successful or happier than they are.

We all want to believe in the concept of happy families, but this idea can actually be detrimental to a person's overall mental health. If you genuinely believe that everyone in the family should always get along then you are more likely to blame yourself when family tensions arise.

Saturday 26 April 1997

I had a difficult day today. There was something that I wanted to say to Mum but I just felt too nervous. I didn't know how she would take it. I was worried that she would feel hurt by my comments. I thought she would probably be very difficult. I realized that I was scared of her and her reaction, and that I just couldn't talk honestly with her.

She'd said to me the day before that if I needed any help I just had to ask, so I thought I'd try today. However, the look on her face the moment I started to speak made it impossible for me to go on and I gave up. So now I feel like both a failure and a coward.

I mentioned earlier how important it is to be honest in your diary. It may be easier to keep denying the truth to yourself but this will not help with your recovery.

Friday 5 September 1997

I felt very scared this morning because I'd agreed to try a piece of spinach and ricotta quiche. I was not only frightened of eating the food but I was also worried about how I would feel after the meal. Something extra happened though, which complicated things even further. I found that I really liked the taste of the quiche and that scared me.

One of the excuses I've used for years to avoid eating certain foods is that I didn't like the taste because people don't make you eat what you don't like. I can't quite explain why finding out I like a food is frightening but I know that it is.

Many sufferers feel as though they are being controlled by a 'voice' in their head which directs them and tells them how to behave. I experienced this and often found it helpful to write about the 'voice' in my diary.

Monday 3 November 1997

I feel lonely and hopeless at the moment. I looked at other people and saw them as successes, whereas I am just a failure. To cover up this pain, I started exercising.

I tried a new exercise I'd never done before and I did it over and over again until my legs were really shaking. Now I feel very stiff but that pain feels good because my mind is saying – 'The pain shows how hard you worked. Exercise is good and food is bad. Exercise more and eat even less.'

I know I shouldn't listen to this voice in my head and allow it to control me but it is so loud and strident. It is always shouting at me.

Sometimes it can be helpful just to write about how hard things are feeling in general. It does not have to be triggered by any special event. Eating disorders are illnesses which cause depression and this can be extremely difficult for sufferers to cope with.

Sunday 16 November 1997

I am scared right now because I feel out of control. Up to this point, I had always been able to block out the emotional pain even though it was intense. I could appear fine on the outside even though I was hurting inside. I can't seem to do that any more and that's what is so frightening.

I'm scared that this pain is all that I am. It feels so intense – as if it fills the whole of me. Strangely, I worry that if it did go, I'd just be this empty shell of a person.

The more that you express your feelings in the diary, the easier it will become to be open about your emotions. It is never easy to start writing down your innermost feelings, which are complicated and frequently painful. However, you can also write about the happier events in your life. Even in the most difficult life, there are times when good things happen or you experience moments of happiness.

When you record these thoughts, it is important not to put a negative spin on a good event or to rewrite it differently later to fit in with your mood at the time of writing. If you are feeling depressed or hopeless, it is often tempting to twist positive events into appearing negative. This is not possible – if a good thing happens in your life, it will always remain good even if you are experiencing emotional or physical problems.

An example from my life was when I passed my driving test despite it being a particularly traumatic period for me. I can still remember the total joy I felt at hearing the news that I had passed.

Wednesday 21 May 1997

I still can't actually believe I passed my driving test today. It was a really long test (40 minutes) and we went a long distance outside the town.

I was nervous and shaking the whole time but when we turned back into the test centre, the examiner said 'It's OK. You can smile now. Go on – smile.'

I had to sign my name on the pass certificate and it was all crooked because my writing was so shaky. Finally I'll now be able to get my own car.

If you think that you would like to try writing a thoughts and feelings diary then start immediately. Write down all that you've felt today. Try not to focus purely on the events of the day but, rather, on how those events made you feel and what thoughts were present at the time.

Remember that you do not have to buy an expensive diary for this exercise – a cheap school-style notebook is just as good. It may be that you find this form of therapy beneficial and keep the diary for months or years. My own diaries chart the progress of my recovery and were very helpful to read if I needed encouragement to keep moving forward.

Chapter 6

Cognitive Behaviour Therapy

Cognitive behaviour therapy (CBT) is recognized as a successful therapy tool for eating disorder sufferers. The theory behind this approach is that our thoughts directly affect our feelings, which, in turn, control how we behave. Thinking negative thoughts about ourselves can lead to a drop in self-esteem, which results in people turning to negative behaviours such as fasting or self-harming to try and control these feelings.

The aim of CBT is to identify the negative thoughts which result in negative behaviour. When these thoughts are isolated, sufferers then learn how to turn the negative thoughts into positive ones. This will then cause them to feel more positive, which will lead them to behave in a kinder way towards themselves.

Research has shown that our brains analyse and interpret what we see, hear, feel, touch and taste before we are even conscious of it happening. This interpretation is a kind of internal conversation that we conduct with ourselves (often referred to as 'self-talk').

People who are suffering from anxiety or depressive conditions such as eating disorders have a negative internal mind-set. They are continually reminding themselves about fears and insecurities relating to their own lives, the world and the future. It is these constant negative thoughts which cause their depressed moods, resulting in self-destructive behaviour and an inability to cope.

For example, you get into a car and it will not start. Instant reaction: 'Damn – I'll have to call the garage.'

This response shows natural annoyance but also displays an ability to cope. A plan is already formed to solve the problem.

Negative reaction: 'Oh no! The car won't start! What am I going to do? This is typical – everything always goes wrong for me! I can't take this! It's all too much!'

These negative thoughts overwhelm the person, leaving him or her feeling hopeless and unable to cope with a normal everyday situation. These thoughts are known as negative automatic thoughts (NATS).

Defining negative automatic thoughts

There are four criteria that define these destructive thoughts.

- *They are always negative.* The clue to discovering a real negative thought is that it would depress anyone who *believed* it.

- *They are automatic.* They appear instantly in your head. You do not have to try and manufacture them.

- *They are short and familiar.* They will be in your own words and are statements which you have created. There is no logical reasoning behind them and they are often rude and insulting (e.g. 'I am a failure', 'I'm an ugly fat pig', 'I'm a stupid cow').

- *They are distorted.* The thoughts are not based on facts or reality but are twisted logic that is deliberately designed to make you feel unhappy.

Eating disorder sufferers often experience NATS. These thoughts are usually about themselves – their bodies, behaviour and eating habits. They cause a drop in self-esteem and lead sufferers to feel hopeless about their situation. Learning to challenge these thoughts can lift sufferers' mood, improve their sense of self-worth and give them a more hopeful outlook.

The first step in CBT is to identify your own personal NATS. Everyone experiences negative thoughts from time to time and they can often appear very persuasive. For example:

I am a failure – nothing I do is ever good enough.

I'm getting older and losing my looks. No one will love me.

I always eat too much. I'm a greedy pig.

People don't really like me – they are just being kind.

I know that eating just a few extra calories could cause my NATS to start. Many of my low moods were also triggered by feelings of being a failure. My mother always singled out my brother for praise since we were children. This left me feeling inadequate and unworthy as a daughter. Even just a few words about how good he was at his job eventually triggered my NATS. This led to feelings of hopelessness and I would cut down on my food intake as a result since I learnt to believe that I did not deserve the nourishment.

Exercise 6.1

NATS

Try and list some of your own negative thoughts. If you don't think you have any, wait until the next time you are feeling sad, depressed or upset. What are you thinking? What went through your mind just before you felt sad?

My negative automatic thoughts

_____

_____

_____

_____

_____

_____

_____

_____

_____

_____

_____

Negative thoughts also often occur in groups, with one thought triggering another. If you are in a low mood, it is likely that you can identify a whole string of negative thoughts which are all occurring at the same time. For example: Christine overslept and was late for work. The following is the negative chain of thoughts which led her to then binge and vomit at lunchtime.

I am useless. I never get anything right. My boss will hate me. Everyone in the office will think I'm lazy. No one will like me. I'll be alone for the rest of my life. I'm wasting this job opportunity. I'll end up getting fired. Why am I trying to diet? I'll have no job and no friends. There's no point being thin. I might as well have a burger and fries at lunchtime and stuff them in my stupid fat face. I hate myself so much.

This downwards spiral of thought began with a small insignificant incident, which grew bigger and bigger until Christine hated herself and engaged in destructive behaviour. If she could have stopped this train of thought in its early stages, it would have prevented a great deal of emotional pain.

It will feel difficult to write down your thoughts at first. You may feel swept along by a low mood and either forget to write them down or feel too upset to do so. Practice is the key to identifying your thoughts. Even if you can not write them down as they happen, take some time to list them as soon as you feel able.

CBT utilizes thoughts and moods charts to help sufferers identify their negative thoughts. Initially, patients will use four-column thoughts and moods charts and, as they progress in their recovery, they move on to the six-column thoughts and moods charts.

Four-column thoughts and moods charts

The aim of these charts is to help the sufferer record the following.

- *The date*. In this column, you list when the situation occurred.

- *The emotions*. In this column, you list what feelings you are experiencing. For example, whether you feel hurt, upset, angry, guilty, depressed, anxious, afraid, envious, ashamed, lonely, suicidal and so on. You will sometimes find that you experience more than one emotion at a time. It is important to enter these in your chart if this is the case (such as feeling both hurt and angry).

- *The situation*. In this column, you list what was happening or what you were doing at the time the NATS began. Who were you talking to? Did someone say something which affected your mood?

- *The NATS*. In this column, you list the chain of thoughts which occurred as your mood became negative. It may be that you have a whole stream of negative thoughts and it is important to include them all. Remember that you only record thoughts and not feelings in this particular column.

The difference between feelings and thoughts

If you are having difficulty distinguishing between thoughts and feelings, put these words in front of each sentence: 'I feel …' and 'I think …'. 'I feel …' will always be followed by only one or two words, such as 'I feel sad' or 'I feel lonely'. These are statements of fact and they cannot be argued with.

'I think …' is a more complicated statement since thoughts are more descriptive by their very nature (such as 'I think that I am a horrible person and that no one likes me'). This statement is *not* a fact and it can be challenged with logic.

This very important distinction between feelings and thoughts is the central principle of CBT. It is sometimes possible to confuse thoughts and feelings. This error is shown in the statement: 'I *feel* that I am all alone in the world.' This is actually a negative belief and *not* a feeling. The sentence should read 'I *think* that I am all alone in the world.'

Once you have identified the separate thoughts and feelings in a sentence then they can be challenged using CBT. For example, the following sentence shows a distinct thought and feeling (the feeling here occurs as a reaction to the thought).

> I *feel* lonely because I *think* that I have no friends and am all alone.

It is also important not to record thoughts as questions because this makes them harder to challenge with positive responses. For example:

> 'Why am I a failure?' should be written as the NAT: 'I am a failure.'

> 'Why am I always doing everything wrong?' should be written as the NAT: 'I am always doing everything wrong.'

These negative statements should then be recorded on the sheets so that they can then be challenged.

I have included here one of my own four-column thoughts and moods charts, which I filled in during therapy. As a child, I had been treated badly by family members which led me to grow up trying to please everyone. I had an intense fear of making people angry and this came across in my entries.

Date	Emotions	Situation	NAT
26 August 1996	Miserable (80%)	Dad looking cross. Mum says it's due to Mark coming down	I think it must be my fault. I must have said or done something wrong (100%)
26 August 1996	Scared (90%)	Feeling ill	Don't want to admit how I feel in case it worries somebody. I don't want to be a nuisance (100%)
27 August 1996	Miserable and tearful (95%)	Didn't manage to eat as much as I wanted to	I am so disappointed in myself. I am a failure (100%)

Copy out a blank version of this chart and fill in some of your own negative thoughts. Try and rate them as a percentage – decide how strongly you believe the thought. If you believe it completely then it should be 100 per cent.

However, if there is some doubt in your mind as to whether the thought is actually true, this should be reflected in your score. It can help aid recovery if you complete these forms on a regular basis.

Challenging your negativity

Once you have become used to the four-column chart, it is time to move on a stage. The next step in CBT is for sufferers to challenge these negative thoughts. At the moment, you believe the negative thoughts which distort your perceptions and make your life feel worse than it actually is. By challenging them, you will be able to see your problems and the world in general more clearly.

The first step in challenging a thought comes by actually working out what the NAT means. Sufferers will often have a general thought, such as 'I think that I am fat,' and to challenge this they will need to define the thought.

For example, Christine thought: 'I'm a fat pig.' When she asked herself what that meant though, she responded more accurately: 'Jane gave me a chocolate bar this morning and now I think I'm a fat pig because I ate it.'

Now that the NAT has been defined, it is possible to challenge the idea. The recovering sufferer aims to find a more constructive and realistic way of looking at the issue. In Christine's example, she could now challenge her thought with the following statements.

Everyone is allowed treats. Chocolate is *not* a bad food. It's a tasty snack which I am allowed. I'm not a pig – I'm a normal person who ate a normal snack. Everyone else in the office is eating chocolate and I can too.

Six key questions

It is not always easy for sufferers to begin challenging their negativity. I know that I found it very difficult at first. My therapists encouraged me to challenge my negative thoughts by asking myself six questions whenever my mood dropped. It is unlikely that all six questions will apply to every situation though (you are likely to find two or three helpful at any one time).

Question 1: What are the fears?

At this point, you need to become a detective and search for evidence against the negative thought. Can you remember any time when the NAT was not true?

This is the most helpful question to ask yourself since just thinking of times when the NAT was not true can help to lighten your mood immediately.

Typical negative thoughts which can be challenged with this question are sweeping statements, such as:

> I do everything wrong.

> I am hated by everyone.

> My life is in ruins – nothing ever goes right.

If sufferers think along these lines, their mood will instantly drop. However, gathering evidence by asking follow-up questions and replying honestly can help to improve it again.

- Do you really do everything wrong?

- Was there literally nothing at all that went well this week?

Once you start to investigate, you will be able to accumulate a whole list of positive statements, such as:

- Received a birthday card and present.

- Drove a friend home from work.

Listing even simple everyday tasks like doing the washing or making your bed helps to counter sweeping negative statements such as 'I do everything wrong.'

Question 2: Am I trying to be perfect?

Our standards are often set too high and this usually results in feeling a failure. Ask yourself how close you came to succeeding. Would someone else have classed the same event as a success rather than a failure?

Eating disorder sufferers are frequently perfectionists and this causes them to be extremely self-critical. Examine your negative thoughts – are they linked to a need to be perfect? Some examples:

> I made a spelling mistake in a letter. It's ruined. I'm so useless.
>
> I didn't make my bed this morning. I'm a failure. My house is a mess.
>
> I didn't eat my meal at 1 pm. It's spoilt now. I can't eat it at all.

Would you expect other people to reach the high standards that you set for yourself?

It can also help to ask yourself: 'Who am I trying to please?' High standards are often a byproduct of a difficult childhood and experiences of critical adults.

Challenge your own standards – one spelling mistake does not ruin a letter for example. Observe other people and see if they are less critical of themselves. If they are, it is likely that they feel happier and more at ease with themselves on a day to day basis because they are not filling their heads with negative self-talk.

Question 3: Was it really that bad?

Some events can feel disastrous but they are rarely as bad as we think. Negative thoughts tend to get exaggerated so that a small incident can feel like a crisis. Examples of this type of NAT include:

> This is the end of the world. My life is over.
>
> I'm falling apart. I just can't cope.
>
> I behaved badly and people will hate me.

Everyone exaggerates at times, and when you are in a low mood it is easy to get drawn into worst-case scenarios. Challenge these thoughts by asking yourself: 'Am I making a mountain out of a molehill?' or 'If the incident happened to someone else, would I still think it was the end of the world?'

These types of extreme worst-case scenarios are often referred to as 'catastrophic negative thoughts'. They can also be challenged by confronting them with the next question.

Question 4: How much do I want this to affect my life?

How important is this negative thought? If you find that negative thoughts are affecting you for long periods of time, this can be an effective question to ask.

These are some examples of this kind of long-term negative thinking:

> I was so hurt by their comments that my entire day was ruined.

> I ate two pieces of cake and felt like the fattest cow on earth for days.

> The whole week was ruined because of what happened.

Everyone experiences difficult and unpleasant events – how we deal with them is a good indicator of our mental health. Panicking or allowing events to totally overshadow your life is extremely unhealthy. All problems can be dealt with in a positive manner, and lessons can be learnt which teach you valuable coping strategies.

For example, Jane owns her own shop. On one occasion, a customer was rude and abrasive because she had accidentally given him the wrong change. Her immediate reaction was to think: 'I am so useless. This is all my fault. I'll have to shut down the business. This has ruined my life.'

Gradually, though, she stopped feeling so upset and began to work at the problem by telling herself: 'Everyone makes mistakes. That customer did not need to be so rude. I meant to give the correct change and I rectified the mistake as soon as I was aware of it. I'm not going to let this upset me. I very rarely make an error. I run a good business.'

As Jane repeated these words to herself, she started to feel better and realized that she had overdramatized the situation. The customer had moved on with his life and was not dwelling on this one minor incident and neither should she.

Question 5: Am I really to blame for this situation?

People who are responsible for others at home, school or work can blame them-selves for other people's behaviour (such as a child feeling responsible for her parents' divorce or a manager feeling total responsibility for his staff). Some people also feel liable for events which are not their responsibility and accept the blame for the actions of others.

I have done this for much of my own life and it is very convenient for the people around, since it means that there is always a convenient scape-goat. I am lucky now to have a partner who does not allow me to take the blame for things which are not my responsibility.

Are you taking too much responsibility for other people's behaviour when it is actually outside your control? The following are examples of this kind of negative thought.

> If I had been a better child, my parents would not be divorcing now.

> If I had kept a closer eye on my team at work, stock would not have gone missing.

By challenging these negative beliefs, a rational plan can be drawn up.

A manager may be responsible for his staff but he also has to trust them. He cannot watch them constantly since this would make working conditions impossible and the staff discontent. He therefore has to use his own discretion. Things may occasionally go missing but the overall morale of his entire staff is of greater importance. It is vital for him to accept his limitations and recognize that each member of his staff is ultimately responsible for his or her own behaviour.

Question 6: How would this appear to someone else?

It is worth considering how a situation might seem to a different person. You may also try asking yourself how you would have coped with the situation yourself before you were ill.

These two questions can be very helpful if you have reacted in an extreme manner to a situation. If you watch other people coping with similar events, you are likely to see a calmer response. If you can, try talking to them about how they felt during the situation and how they have learnt to deal with it.

The following example demonstrates how different people can view a situation in two completely different ways.

> Julie met a couple of friends (Lisa and Jane) for a coffee in town. Lisa was her usual chirpy self, chatting about her work and boyfriend. However, Jane was sullen and quiet, only joining in when she was asked a direct question. Julie then began to feel concerned and negative thoughts started to plague her on the way home: 'I've upset Jane. She didn't want to talk with me. She must hate me. Everyone hates me.'
>
> After a miserable few hours, Julie phoned Lisa and said that she was worried. Lisa's response was that she thought Jane probably just had some problem of her own on her mind. Julie was amazed at how

cheerful Lisa still sounded. She had not been concerned about Jane's behaviour and certainly did not think that it might have been her own fault.

The next day, Julie learnt that Jane's mother had been taken into hospital but that she did not want to talk about it during the meeting. Julie realized how ridiculous it was that she had spent hours worrying about something she might have done wrong and tried to learn from Lisa's attitude instead.

It is easy to jump to the wrong conclusion or make assumptions about a situation where you do not have all the facts. Talk to the people around you when you have concerns and they will often be able to help alleviate your worries.

Six-column thoughts and moods charts

Now that you know how to define a negative thought and you have a list of questions to challenge them with, it is time to move on to the six-column thoughts and moods charts. These consist of the following columns.

- date

- emotions

- situation

- NATS

- rational answer

- outcome.

In these larger charts, you also enter the rational answer to your negative thoughts. Use the six questions to help you build up positive responses, then rate how much you believe your rational positive answer as a percentage.

Do not be disappointed if at first you do not feel that you believe it. This is a common reaction and gradually you will begin to believe the positive responses rather than the NATS as you progress with your CBT.

You complete each entry by filling in the outcome section, which is divided into three sub-sections:

- How far do you now believe the negative thought? (0–100%)

As time passes and you learn to challenge your negative thoughts as soon as they occur, this figure should steadily drop.

- How do you feel now? (0–100%)

Look at your earlier percentage listed in the 'Emotions' column. Have your feelings improved? The stronger you believe your positive rational answers, the more your mood will improve.

- What can you do now that is positive and constructive?

This final section asks you to do something which is both constructive and positive. It can relate to the problem or it can be something completely separate. This can also act as a distraction technique.

The following is one of my own mood diary entries, to give you an idea of how they should look.

Date	30 October 1997
Emotions	Worried and upset (95%)
Situation	Mum saying that I've affected everyone else's eating
NAT	I'm such a nuisance for causing so much bother
Rational answer	I am not responsible for other people's behaviour. It is up to them what they do. I can only cope with my own eating (4%)
Outcome	1. (96%), 2. (90%), 3. Write some Christmas cards

Now it is time for you to fill in some six-column thoughts and moods charts of your own. Copy out a blank version of this chart and add in any problems you experience and your responses to them on a regular basis.

Exercise 6.2

Thought awareness

Thoughts are not facts. We often assume that every thought we have must be given credence and taken seriously. This is not the case, however.

Write down all the thoughts you have over a specific period of time. This can be anything from a minute to an hour. When you have a list of all your thoughts during this period (which is likely to be quite a long list), try answering the following questions.

- *Which of the thoughts did you take seriously?*

It is common for people to believe their negative thoughts more strongly than the positive ones, which are frequently dismissed. A person can hear hundreds of positive comments about him- or herself and only a few negative remarks yet it is likely that these are the ones which they will always remember.

- *Which thoughts affect your mood?*

Eating disorder sufferers are strongly affected by thoughts of food and weight. These thoughts can alter their mood, depending on whether they feel that an event is good or bad. A drop in weight can lead to a feeling of euphoria and happy thoughts. However, any weight gain can cause sufferers to criticize themselves harshly and fill their head with negativity.

- *Did any of your thoughts affect your behaviour or cause you to change your plans?*

Anxiety attacks can leave a sufferer feeling frightened and isolated. A dinner invitation could bring on such an attack. Negative thoughts concerning the evening may lead a sufferer to feel unable to attend and he or she may choose to stay home rather than joining the party.

- *Were you able to ignore any of your thoughts?*

As sufferers progress with CBT, they find that they are able to begin ignoring many of their more outlandish thoughts, which seemed perfectly normal before the treatment began.

Repeat this exercise once a month and you should be able to see changes begin to happen. As you learn to replace negative thoughts with positive ones, you will find that your behaviour is no longer totally controlled by your negativity.

Taking back control

The impact of thoughts and memories depends upon how seriously you take them. Much of my recovery was based on dismissing the eating-disordered thoughts as wrong.

I also decided that I was not going to be a victim. I had been abused by a number of different people at various stages in my life but I was no longer going to allow this to hold me back.

Thoughts have as much weight and impact as you choose to give them and, though it may not always feel like it, you are in charge of them. Controlling your thoughts and how seriously you take them is the real control that you can exert over your eating disorder.

Chapter 7

Exposure Therapy

Exposure therapy is a behavioural therapy process during which patients confront a feared situation, object, memory or thought. By facing these situations, they will gradually reduce the anxiety they experience.

Exposure therapy can be carried out in real, everyday situations (known as 'in vivo' exposure) or it can be experienced through imaginary situations (such as 'virtual' or 'imaginal' exposure).

Depending on the patient and the level of anxiety he or she is experiencing, exposure therapy can be carried out at two different speeds:

- *Graded (or graduated) exposure.* This involves introducing the patient to the feared situation very gradually. This allows the patient to experience anxiety, although not to a level that feels unbearable. This procedure is also known as 'systemic desensitization'.

- *Flooding.* This involves introducing the patient to the feared situation all at once. The patient is then encouraged to remain in the situation until his or her anxiety starts to subside.

Exposure therapy is a safe treatment method, although patients naturally tend to prefer the graduated approach. All of the exercises in this chapter will use the graduated method of exposure therapy.

The purpose of treatment is to reduce a sufferer's level of anxiety so that it is either manageable (known as 'habituation') or disappears completely (known as 'extinction').

Exposure therapy usually begins with sufferers making a list of all their feared situations, which is called a 'hierarchy'.

Exercise 7.1

Feared situations

List all of the situations that you find fearful and give each one a
number (with '0' representing the least fearful and '100' as the most
frightening). This is known as the 'subjective units of distress scale'
(SUDS).

Different types of exposure therapy

Patient-directed exposure

This is the simplest form of the treatment and involves sufferers working on their
own. Once they have made their list of fearful situations (either alone or with a
therapist's help) they then begin to work through the list at their own speed. They
should also keep a note of their experiences on the chart.

It is recommended that a session of exposure therapy is carried out every day
until the patient's anxiety is reduced. Sufferers should begin with the fearful
situation which produces the least anxiety. They are to carry out this action or
behaviour once a day until they can perform it without feeling anxious.

This may take a number of days or weeks so it is important for sufferers to
remain patient. Once they have tackled one listed item, it is then time to move on
to another.

If sufferers have a therapist who is helping them to tackle the problem, they
can discuss their progress during the sessions. Although it is always beneficial to
have help from a therapist, it is possible for sufferers to utilize this approach by
themselves or with help from family and friends.

As mentioned above, patient-directed exposure is viewed as a safe form of
therapy since it is taken at a gentle pace and the patient is in control. If at any point
patients experience too much anxiety, they can stop the session and try again
when they are feeling more at ease.

Therapist-assisted exposure

In this form of treatment, the therapist is with the patient when the patient is
exposed to his or her feared situation. The therapist can then give help and advice
to sufferers when they are feeling at their most anxious. This can be a more

intensive approach since the therapist will often challenge the sufferer to experience a larger number of anxiety-inducing tasks.

Therapists will talk to sufferers and help them to deal with any irrational thoughts they may be experiencing. They may also use relaxation techniques (such as creative visualization and breathing exercises) to keep their patient calm.

I underwent a variety of different exposure therapy exercises during my treatment. Although they did cause me to feel a greater level of anxiety in the short term, they proved increasingly beneficial as time went by. Breaking the rigid rules of my disorder and confronting my fears one at a time allowed me to make real progress.

On one occasion, I spent the morning baking a cake with an occupational therapist. This exercise was to allow me to accept that high-fat foods were not 'bad' or forbidden.

Another exercise was going supermarket shopping with a psychiatric nurse. This task was planned because I had become unable to purchase anything but the lowest-calorie foods. We walked around the shop, carefully placing higher-calorie foods in the trolley. All the while, my therapist was helping me to cope with the panic that confronting this fear was producing.

Group exposure therapy

These sessions usually include group education, individual exposure therapy tasks and then group discussions about the feelings experienced. It can be very beneficial and comforting to talk with others who are experiencing similar anxieties. Even though the feared situations are different, the emotional responses and anxieties are often exactly the same for everyone.

PANIC ATTACKS

Specific conditions have different kinds of exposure therapy designed for them. Eating disorder sufferers experience strong feelings of panic when they are faced with even a small amount of food. This can, in turn, lead some patients to become afraid of this fear itself and of having panic attacks in public. It is often important for sufferers to begin by tackling this problem.

Panic attacks can make sufferers feel dizzy, sweaty and out of breath as their heart rate increases. The therapist encourages sufferers to recreate these feelings so that they can accept how they feel without taking any action to control them.

Spinning around can make a person feel dizzy and running on the spot increases the heart rate.

Once sufferers are experiencing symptoms similar to a panic attack, the therapist explains that they will not come to any harm as a result of these feelings. They are not in any danger and these are not the symptoms of heart problems. They do not need to try and escape. If they remain calm, the feelings will just pass on their own (deep breathing exercises can also help in calming down). Recognizing this should help remove the fear that panic attacks lead to serious consequences and that they need to 'escape' when one happens.

If you feel panicked at the idea of introducing new foods into your diet, it would be beneficial to remember and to practise this technique. It should be repeated until sufferers can accept that the symptoms of panic are not harmful. They can then take the next step, which is to introduce a situation which is likely to involve a food that they have been avoiding. Again, repeat the panic technique to show that the fear itself is not as big an obstacle as you might have thought.

This particular exposure therapy treatment for panic attacks has proved to be very successful with patients. Studies have shown that between 50 per cent and 90 per cent of all patients experienced relief from their feelings of panic as a result.

Results of exposure therapy

It does appear that continual daily exposure is the most effective way of treating anxiety disorders. Although patients usually prefer the gradual exposure methods to the flooding treatment, they both seem to be equally effective.

For exposure therapy to work, it must be completely voluntary and patients need to understand that they can end the exposure at any time during the therapy. Every time sufferers complete a treatment and choose *not* to escape from the situation they are in, they weaken their illness and lower their anxiety levels.

During each session, patients should experience the maximum anxiety that they are able to accept at that point. When sufferers recognize that they are feeling calmer during an exercise, this is an indication that they are ready to move on to the next task on their hierarchy list. Sometimes relaxation techniques are taught by therapists so that patients can use them during the more stressful parts of their treatment.

In recent years, there have been significant developments in this area of treatment. Virtual reality exposure therapy, for example, allows patients to participate in a computer-generated environment. They can then be exposed to their fears in a virtual world and this approach has proved successful since it allows patients to feel more in control of their environment.

Now it is time to start working through your list of fearful situations. Remember that this is a hierarchy so begin at the bottom of the list. Ideally, you need to carry out this task once a day for a two-week period until you no longer feel anxious. If you remain calm while doing this in less time then move on to the next task.

Possible exposure therapy tasks

If you are having trouble deciding on some exercises for your list, consider trying some of the ones below.

- Introduce one new food into your diet and make sure that you include this in your eating plan every day for two weeks (or until you feel comfortable with eating it).

- Not all of your negative behaviours will relate to food. You may have become obsessed with certain routines since your eating disorder developed. Select a chore which you always complete each day (such as washing up straight after a meal) and then put that task off for a set number of hours.

- Introduce a 'grazing between meals' system. Have small bowls of finger food in places where you can pick at them. These are in addition to your normal foods and you must not cut out any other calories to compensate for them.

- Social situations can be difficult for eating disorder sufferers. It may be that you have become isolated during your illness. Try to pick an anxiety-inducing event or situation which will progress your recovery. See if you can meet up with a friend for an hour or two. Shopping can feel intimidating to some so plan to buy an item from a store. It does not have to be anything expensive – a newspaper only costs a few pence.

- You may also find it difficult to make telephone calls. I know that this was a source of anxiety for me. Try to make one telephone call each day until the anxiety starts to fade.

Chapter 8

Triggers and How to Deal with Them

What are triggers?

Triggers are considered by eating disorder sufferers to be the situations or events which cause them to lapse into negative behaviour such as disordered eating, laxative abuse, overexercising, self-harming or vomiting. Most sufferers will quickly be able to give a list of their most common triggers. It is important to recognize what can tip a sufferer over the edge and plan strategies for dealing with these.

However, stop for a moment and try looking at the whole issue of triggers more objectively. The basic idea of recovery is to take responsibility for your eating disorder. Say to yourself: 'I am in control of my own life and I have the power to beat my illness.'

It is often more comfortable to blame others for your negative behaviour. For example, a sufferer once said to me: 'I haven't eaten all day but that's not my fault. A friend told me she was dieting and that triggered me.'

It is far easier to pass on the responsibility. In the above case, the sufferer needed to accept that her friend's comments led to her feeling guilty for eating, *but* that it should not have affected her eating plan for that day.

When you are recovering, there will always be people around you who are on diets. Our society is becoming increasingly health conscious and adverts for low-calorie foods and new diets appear to be everywhere. If you know that these images and ideas affect you strongly, try having a strategy in place for dealing with these triggers in a positive way. For example, counteract the feelings that are triggered with some positive thoughts such as:

Julie is on a diet because she feels that she has to watch her weight. I do not need to diet. I need to follow my healthy eating plan.

Everyone is different and they need to eat different types and amounts of food. I need to follow my special food plan and then I will recover from my eating disorder.

Remember that you cannot control what other people may say and do but you can control your reaction to it. Start by making a list of your most common triggers. These were some of mine:

- A meal out where I had no idea exactly how many calories I had eaten.

- Social situations with friends and family that involved food.

- Eating more food than I felt I should have done.

- Weigh-in sessions at the doctor's.

Now try listing your key triggers (see Exercise 8.1).

When you know exactly what your triggers are then you can work out various coping strategies. It may be that you need to ask for help from your therapist or a friend to work out solutions to some of the difficult situations that you face.

For example, dealing with my issues at weigh-in times involved my speaking with the healthcare professionals that I was seeing. A pound up or down on the scales could determine how much I would allow myself to eat the following week. It was therefore decided that I would be weighed while facing backwards instead.

At first, this seemed like a terrible idea since I believed that I needed to know my weight. However, it gradually became a relief not to worry about what the scales would say each day. I no longer adjusted my diet in response to the fluctuating readings and I began to make some real progress.

A common trigger for most sufferers is the media, and especially magazines. The images in magazines can lead to an increased feeling of dissatisfaction with your own body and a strong desire to diet.

- Do you find yourself comparing your body to those of the models and celebrities in these magazines?

- How does this affect your mood?

- Does it result in you eating less that day?

Exercise 8.1

My triggers

_____

_____

_____

_____

_____

_____

_____

_____

_____

_____

I have looked into many of these publications and it is interesting to note how many use post-production techniques to digitally enhance their pictures. Photographs are frequently airbrushed out to create a more 'perfect' image. Camera angles, lighting techniques and make-up all help celebrities and models to look their best in magazines and on television.

Try the following activity to give yourself a more realistic idea of how women actually look today.

Go to a busy high street and take a look at the size of women that you see there. Approximately 60 per cent of women are currently a UK size 16 (US size 14) or above. Make an honest assessment. Do you see any women that are the current size of models?

Unfortunately, if you do actually spot an extremely thin young woman then it is likely that she is also suffering from disordered eating or is ill in some other way. Women's bodies are not supposed to be the size of models. If you do reach this size, it is likely that your periods would have stopped since your body knows that it is at an unhealthy weight and would be unable to produce a healthy child.

If you feel pressured by the idealized images of women in magazines, it is also worth asking yourself whether you should be allowing other people to tell you what it is that you want. Given a free choice, would you really choose to spend valuable time aspiring to look like someone else?

Many sufferers have told me that they find it difficult to cope with knowing the weight of other sufferers. Anorexia (and to some extent bulimia) are competitive illnesses, with the sufferer feeling a strong need to be the thinnest in the group. This can lead to some problems in eating disorder units. Although it is important for patients to learn that they need not compete with others in their unit, this understanding often comes later in recovery.

However, sufferers can often help one another as well. One unit that I was staying in placed a newly admitted sufferer together with one in the later stages of recovery so that they could help each other. The newer patient reminded the other how debilitating an eating disorder was and the nearly recovered patient showed how positive recovery could be.

Food plans are another potential trigger in hospital units. In the unit I was in, we all had different meal plans tailored to meet our needs. However, this did cause some problems since the patients would compare calorie content in the food plans and want to swap meals.

Mealtimes could also be problematic since difficult behaviour from one sufferer could influence all of the others. I eventually asked to eat with non-eating-disordered patients since I found it beneficial to see how people with healthy attitudes towards food behaved during mealtimes:

The next exercise tackles the problem of eating with people who make comments about certain foods and refer to them as 'bad', which I found to be a potential trigger. An example from my diaries.

> *Trigger*: I am sitting in a café watching two women eat low-calorie food. After they finish their salad, one woman says, 'Now I am going to be really naughty and have a cake.'

> *Resulting thoughts*: I felt that it was wrong to eat high-calorie food and that I was never allowed to eat cakes.

Triggers are going to be all around you when you begin recovery and potentially each one could cause you to relapse but remember that you are really in control. A magazine, a thoughtless comment or an advert can only affect you if you allow it

Exercise 8.2

Healthy eating

Plan to have a meal with a friend or relative who has a healthy balanced diet. Observe how he ors she eats foods from each group – proteins, carbohydrates, fruits, vegetables and even high-fat treats. Perhaps have a discussion about how a healthy diet can include a little of everything.

to. Take responsibility for your own recovery and learn to fight back against these triggers.

One of my most frequent triggers was the belief that I had upset someone or done something wrong. This would always cause me to punish myself through self-harming or starvation. I learned to use CBT to help myself discover the truth about each situation. Had I really done something wrong or was it just an unsubstantiated feeling?

For example, I often felt that I had eaten too much. I could experience this guilt after eating just one chocolate. Rather than giving in to this feeling and overexercising, I learned to challenge the irrational thought instead. 'Normal' people could eat half a dozen chocolates without feeling guilt. I had not done anything wrong by eating only one and I did not need to punish myself.

Exercise 8.3

Triggers

Try going back to your list of triggers (Exercise 8.1) and challenging them one by one.

Triggers are disruptive because they upset a sufferer's feeling of being in control. People usually develop an eating disorder as a way of trying to introduce some control into a life that feels chaotic and frightening. A teenager whose parents are divorcing feels that she is unable to hold her family together but at least she can control what she eats.

The control that sufferers feel they have over food is false, however. Very soon it is the eating disorder which controls the sufferers and they quickly adopt a series of complex and strict rules to govern their lives. The longer sufferers have had their disorder, the harder it feels to break these rules. A major part of recovery is learning how to break these rules.

A classic problem for eating disorder sufferers is that they can never be thin enough. If they were really in control of their disorders, they would be able to set a fixed target weight and stop once they had reached that point. However, it does not work that way in reality. Another target is quickly introduced once the first one is achieved and then another after that until they reach such a low weight that someone has to intervene to get them help.

The longer sufferers have their eating disorder, the harder it feels to break these rules. There are rules concerning weight and others about food. As mentioned, no weight is ever low enough but once sufferers have hit one of their low weight targets then this becomes normal and to go above this is breaking the rules.

Take some time to list some of your own rules.

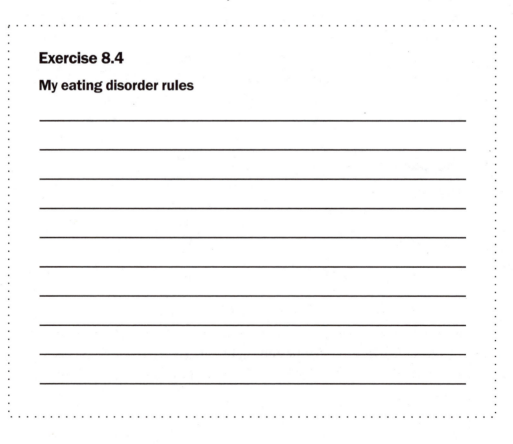

Exercise 8.4

My eating disorder rules

_____

_____

_____

_____

_____

_____

_____

_____

_____

Obsessive compulsive disorder

Eating disorder rules mostly concern food and weight, although sufferers often experience obsessive compulsive disorder (OCD). Both conditions are anxiety disorders and frequently they have developed for the same reasons – usually in an attempt to suppress difficult thoughts, memories and images.

If you feel that you may have OCD traits, try answering the questions below.

- Do you worry about cleanliness and feel concerned about germs?

- Do you have a repeated thought in your head and feel that if you stop worrying about it then something bad will happen?

- Do you ever check and recheck a task even though you know it is completed (e.g. checking doors are locked)?

- Do you feel the need to have a perfectly neat home?

- Do you feel compelled to complete tasks in a specific order?

- Do you frequently have dark thoughts in which you worry that something damaging will happen to you or those you love?

- Do you ever count how often you are performing a task, in the belief that it will keep you safe? For example, some people feel a need to count while washing their hands or they have to touch the doorknob a set number of times before leaving the house.

- Do you feel a need to complete every task perfectly? If you make a mistake, do you restart the task?

- Do you need to have perfect order around you?

- Do you feel angry if someone tries to interfere with or stop your behaviours?

If you have answered 'yes' to a number of these questions, it may be that you are also coping with OCD. It would be worth contacting your doctor to see if there is any help available for you locally.

The following is the story of a young woman who wrote to me about her struggle with both an eating disorder and OCD.

Carrie had suffered from anorexia since her parents separated when she was 14. At 18, she began to realize that she was developing obsessive traits. She felt that she always had to look 'perfect' before she went out and this led to her spending hours in front of the mirror each day.

Her room also had to be 'perfect' with all of her books arranged in alphabetical order. Her clothes were organized by colour, and each item was covered in dry cleaning plastic sheeting to prevent them from getting dusty. Everything had a place and she became very agitated if her mother moved anything. To counteract this anxiety, Carrie started doing all her own cleaning and banned her mother from entering her room.

Carrie's rituals extended to her issues with food as well. She began to prepare all her meals herself and carefully arranged them on the plate, ensuring that no two foods were touching. She always ate her food in a particular order, placing her knife and fork down between each bite.

By the time I had been anorexic for a number of years, I had also accumulated a great many rules which were obsessive in nature. I have listed a number of these below and perhaps you can find some of your own rituals among them.

- Whenever I went out for a meal with my parents, I would only allow myself a jacket potato with baked beans and no butter. I would listen carefully as my father gave the order to make sure that he said 'no butter' and would then check the meal when it arrived.

- I would only have food on my plate that was one level high. This meant that I could not have a pile of peas, for example, because it felt impossible to work out just how many there were.

- If I did not begin my meal at the same time each day then it was ruined and I believed that I could not eat it.

- I ate identical food at each meal every day. Each was eaten at the same speed and needed to last a specific length of time.

- I obsessively read calorie books and knew thousands of food values off by heart. It reached the point at which I could not eat anything unless I knew the calorific value of the food.

Breaking rules

Breaking food- and weight-related rules is difficult and will cause anxiety, although it is very possible. Here are some exercises to try.

Exercise 8.5

Scales

Look at how many times a day you stand on the weighing scales. Keep a count of this for a whole week, writing down the figure for each day below. Remember that honesty is important.

Monday_____

Tuesday_____

Wednesday _____

Thursday_____

Friday _____

Saturday _____

Sunday _____

Take the lowest figure on this list and use it as your new target. This means that next week, you should not weigh yourself more times than this new number.

Carry on like this for another week and then move it down one number for each day the following week. Keep cutting down each week until you are only weighing yourself once a day.

Exercise 8.6

Clothes

Look through the clothes in your wardrobe. Are they all for your actual size or do you have a number of extra-large items? I know that when I was anorexic, I used to bury myself in large sweatshirts and T-shirts in order to hide myself. As you are now starting to recover, it is time to stop hiding from the world.

Choose a T-shirt or top from a shop that is not extra large. It may be that you only feel able to move down to a large size at first but this would still be a good start.

Exercise 8.7

Time

Do you spend a lot of time watching the clock and timing yourself when eating? Many of my own food rituals were based around time. Lunch was from 1.10 to 2.00 pm and I managed to make two slices of bread, one cheese triangle, half an apple and a small chocolate biscuit last for nearly an hour.

One of the exercises a therapist once set me was designed to break this time ritual by shaking up my schedule. Some days I had to start my meal five minutes later than normal and at other times, I had to finish five minutes earlier. Using this method, I gradually managed to break this pattern.

All eating disorder sufferers have different sets of rules for their illnesses. If you have ones that are time-related, try thinking up an exercise of your own which would break these rules one step at a time. If you feel controlled by the clock, for example, you may want to try turning it around while you are eating so that it no longer dominates your mealtimes.

Alternatively, your problem may be that your mealtimes are lasting too long. Anorexia sufferers often eat their food slowly, one tiny bite at a time, and this can mean that meals may take a while. When I was in hospital, we were only allowed 30 minutes per meal so that we learnt to eat at a more normal speed.

If this is the case for you, try setting yourself a time limit for your meals. If you usually take an hour, set the meal time for 55 minutes instead. Do this every day for a week and then reduce the limit to 50 minutes. Keep this up until you are comfortable with eating at a regular pace again.

Exercise 8.8

Mirrors

As an anorexic, I found that I often looked in mirrors to try and reassure myself that I was not as fat as I believed myself to be. However, this did not comfort me and often made me feel depressed and hopeless.

When I moved in with Simon, I suddenly found myself living in a house that had very few mirrors. At first, I found this worrying but quite quickly I began to feel calmer. I was not constantly checking the size of my legs or wondering if my stomach showed. It also gradually helped me to cope with gaining the weight I needed for recovery to take place.

If you find yourself repeatedly checking your appearance in the mirror, try covering it up for a few hours each day. If you can manage this then gradually extend the time period until the mirror is covered for most of the day or perhaps even removed. This exercise can help to dramatically improve your self-esteem as you learn to see yourself as more than just a reflection.

Final thoughts

Fighting against your set rules and triggers will feel difficult at first. These are rituals and responses that you have trained yourself to react to. However, as with all of these processes, the more you persevere the easier it will become.

Hard though it may be to believe at the moment, healthier responses and beliefs do become second nature with practice. While you are ill, the eating disorder is in charge but as you recover, the balance begins to change. You will gradually regain control of your life.

Chapter 9

Dysfunctional Beliefs

Dysfunctional beliefs are a series of distorted ideas and thoughts which cause a person to feel distressed. Most sufferers hold many such beliefs and it is these which keep them firmly entrenched in their eating disorders. In this chapter, I will explore a number of common dysfunctional beliefs and prove how wrong they are, as well as how they can damage self-esteem.

The following is a list I made of some dysfunctional beliefs that I had accepted as true when I was anorexic.

- I am a bad person and therefore deserve to be punished by self-harming and starvation.

- The feeling of satisfaction that I get when I starve myself is good.

- I can recover by myself – I do not need any outside support.

- I will always be anorexic because it is just the way I am.

- People who say nice things to me are only being kind.

- If people are angry with me, that means they must hate me.

- I can not change my anorexic thoughts – they control me.

- In order to be happy, I must succeed in everything that I do.

- If I do not agree with someone then they will hate me for being so outspoken.

- I will always be on my own because no one could ever love me.

Exercise 9.1

Beliefs

Write down a list of your own dysfunctional beliefs. If you are still uncertain about what they are then have a look at the list below since it may be of help. Remember that these are the thoughts which keep you trapped in your eating disorder.

Common dysfunctional eating disorder beliefs

- It is good when I lose weight and very bad if I gain any.

- My eating disorder is my best friend.

- I am a failure if I eat more than a set number of calories each day.

- I do not have an eating disorder – I'm not thin enough.

- If I go to hospital for treatment, they will just make me fat.

- Thin people are more attractive and get the best things in life.

- No one understands what I am going through.

- It is alright to binge so long as I vomit afterwards.

- It is good to take laxatives because they will help me to become thin.

- It is wrong to be large – I must become thinner.

The 'voice'

Eating disorder sufferers often have thoughts like these constantly buzzing around their heads. Many of them state that it feels like a 'voice' continually telling them how important it is that they lose weight. It taunts them if they slip up by eating too much and it screams rude, hurtful remarks at them.

The 'voice' will always lead you down the wrong road. It will tell you that you are 'fat' and 'lazy', ridicule your achievements and try to destroy your self-esteem. Recovery will begin once you can dismiss all of these comments.

The 'voice' can best be fought using CBT. Since everything that it says is negative, you will need to challenge it with positive statements or affirmations.

Even if you do not really believe the affirmations at first, keep repeating them – they are the correct response and you will gradually come to accept them as true.

The following diary extract shows just how powerful the 'voice' was in my head and how its dysfunctional beliefs controlled my behaviour.

Tuesday 27 January 1998

I am a total failure. I cannot make any food decisions. Every time I try to eat something higher calorie, the voice in my head starts shouting at me 'No – you must not *eat high-calorie foods. They are very bad for you and will instantly make you fat.'*

I know that this has become a rule for me but how do I break it? It feels like the truth. I'm sure that if I eat a bar of chocolate, I'll put on huge amounts of weight. Or perhaps I'll just start eating and won't be able to stop because it tastes so nice.

Distorted rules

The 'voice' is responsible for creating dysfunctional beliefs, although this is not the only way that it tries to control your behaviour. Look at the following tricks which it often uses and see if they are familiar. The more you understand about your eating disorder 'voice' (or negative thinking), the easier it will be to fight.

Lying

The 'voice' always chooses to lie. It will say that all other people hate you, which is, of course, untrue. It always tells anorexic sufferers that they are 'fat' and leads them to believe that they need to lose more weight.

'All or nothing' thinking

This is also known as 'black and white' thinking. For example, the 'voice' claims that if you are not 100 per cent perfect at all times, this means that you are a failure.

Playing on your fears

The 'voice' knows what frightens you and uses this to its advantage. It makes comments such as: 'If you eat that, you'll be the size of a house' or 'If you start eating chocolate then you'll totally lose control and will never be able to stop eating.'

Reading minds

The 'voice' frequently tries to convince you that everyone hates you. Instead of talking honestly with others, it encourages you to try reading their minds instead. This is always done with a negative spin so that you conclude that other people are all thinking badly of you.

Labelling

The 'voice' is intensely cruel and will label you on the basis of little or no evidence. For example, one small mistake such as dropping a cup leads it to call you 'clumsy' and 'useless'.

Blaming yourself

The 'voice' will happily allow you to take the blame for everything that goes wrong. It will always encourage you to believe that you are at fault.

Jumping to conclusions

The 'voice' will take one tiny piece of factual information and draw incorrect and exaggerated conclusions from this. This approach also results in 'inductive reasoning', which is the assumption that if something bad happens to you one day then this will continue to happen for the rest of your life. The 'voice' then uses this type of thinking to reinforce its twisted arguments.

Making mountains out of molehills

The 'voice' magnifies the negative aspects of every situation so that it feels catastrophic. Any positive aspects which might have been present are removed.

Setting rules

Most eating disorder sufferers feel that they have to live their lives according to a strict set of rules. The 'voice' is very adept at setting new rules.

Denying there is a problem

The 'voice' tries to convince you that everyone is making a fuss about nothing. It will work hard to make you believe that your eating is not disordered, you are not unwell and you certainly do not need to go into hospital.

Being selfless

The 'voice' will also try to convince you that thinking about yourself to any degree is selfish. It will tell you that you are a failure so do not deserve anything nice and that you should actually be punished instead.

Taking responsibility for everything

The 'voice' tells you that it is your responsibility to keep others happy. If they seem upset then it will be your fault because you have done something wrong.

Believing that the 'voice' is right

Last, the 'voice' will always tell you that it is right. It will say that friends, family and doctors are all lying to you and that you must ignore them completely.

Exercise 9.2

Affirmations

Whether you view dysfunctional beliefs as negative thinking or as an eating disorder 'voice', it is very possible to change this mind-set by using positive affirmations. By now you should have compiled a list of your own dysfunctional beliefs. For this exercise, you will need to create positive affirmations which counter their negativity.

The following is a list of affirmations which helped me to fight my dysfunctional beliefs.

'Feelings and thoughts can not hurt me. They are *not* the truth.'

'I am stronger than the "voice". I will not let it win.'

'My life will take on new meaning once I am on the road to recovery.'

'I will not hate myself any more but I will hate the "voice" and get rid of it forever.'

'People like me because I am a nice person. The "voice" lies to me constantly.'

'It is good to ask for help – it is a brave decision to make.'

'I am not a failure. I am a success and I should be proud of my achievements.'

'I will not surrender my future to an illness.'

'It is OK to make mistakes. I can learn useful lessons from them.'

'I am sick and tired of being controlled – I want to make my own decisions from now on.'

'I am a strong person and I can beat this eating disorder.'

Exercise 9.3

Playing tennis with the 'voice'

If you can practise answering back to your internal 'voice' with positive statements, it will gradually become easier to beat. This visualization exercise allows you to repeatedly fire positive statements at it with the end result being that you win and take back control.

I chose tennis, although you can select any game which you might prefer. If you choose a team game, try to have each player on your team answering with a positive statement. The eating disorder (with its negative 'voice') is on one side of the net and you are on the other, armed with your positive affirmations.

The disorder serves first – 'You're fat and you deserve to feel bad.'

You return serve with a sharp volley – 'I know that I'm *not* "fat" and even if I were overweight, I don't deserve to feel bad. I am learning to treat myself gently because I am a decent person.'

You win the point – Love 15.

The disorder tries to serve an ace – 'Nobody likes you. You will always be on your own.'

This is a trick shot but you still connect with the ball – 'I have evidence that people like me for who I am. I don't need to be ill or ultra thin to gain people's attention.'

You win another point – Love 30.

The score is in your favour and the disorder is severely weakened by the strength of your personality.

The disorder tries a new attack – 'People don't care about you. Anyone who interferes is only trying to make you huge.'

You reply with – 'The support I receive is helping me to grow in confidence and allowing me to express how I feel. With the help of the people who care, I can beat you once and for all.'

You win again – Love 40.

It tries a final shot – 'People stare at you and think you're a freak.'

You are gaining power and dispatch this pathetic shot with accuracy – 'If anyone stares at me, it is because I look ill. I know that I need to fight to regain my health and that's what I'm doing. Then people will notice that I am healthy and confident when they see me.'

You win. Game set and match.

Now play a game against your own eating disorder. Use phrases which are common negative thinking for you as the shots from the disorder. If it is always telling you not to eat chocolate, for example, use this as its opening serve. Fight back with all the positive responses and logic at your command.

Dreams and nightmares

You may not yet have been able to identify all of your dysfunctional beliefs. It can help to examine your dreams and, in particular, any nightmares that you are having. Try to keep a pad and pen by your bed so that you can record your dreams when you wake up (before they start to fade). When you have recorded your dreams for a week, have a look back through them and see if there are any recurring themes.

During the anorexic years, my dreams eventually began to fall into specific categories.

- Dreams in which a weak and vulnerable animal was being brutally injured by someone stronger.

- Dreams where I was confronted with more food than I could possibly eat. I was not allowed to leave any and was forced to eat everything in front of me.

- Dreams in which I never found someone to love me or where he was taken away from me in some way so that I was left alone.

These dreams demonstrated that I believed the following dysfunctional ideas.

- That because I was an abused child, it was right that I should be continually punished as an adult. By the time I was in my teens, I was so certain I deserved to be treated badly that I started hurting myself through starvation and self-harm.

- That food was bad and it was wrong to eat it.

- That I was totally unloveable. The 'voice' had convinced me that I would always be on my own. I had the dysfunctional belief that everyone I met hated me.

The following diary extract describes some of my nightmares and illustrates how I consistently tried to please everyone in my life.

Friday 14 February 1997

I woke up from a dream this morning crying and it left me feeling sad all day. This was the dream: I was taking an exam when my best friend's boyfriend came into the room and sat down beside me. He told me that he was in love with me and I said, 'No, that couldn't be true. Nothing could happen between us because of my friend.'

He told me that everything between them was over and then he kissed me. It felt wonderful to be loved and wanted, but I knew it was wrong. Then we were discovered and suddenly everyone turned against me. They told me that they despised me and said I had to choose between him and them.

My friend threw all of her boyfriend's possessions at me, saying that she hated both him and me. I put on one of his shirts because I felt closer to him and then sat down and cried because I felt so alone and hated. That's when I woke up.

Other dreams I had included:

- Eating soup from a bowl which never emptied so that I could not finish it.

- Being taken in a limousine to feed some ducks but when I arrive, I see that they have all been shot.

- Being forced to eat a can of worms in tomato sauce.

- I am given an enormous meal that fills two whole plates and all I allow myself to eat are the peas.

- I am trying to rescue stray penguins from hunters when I fall into the water with them and start to drown.

- I receive a huge package of chocolates from Belgium, together with a note which says that if I do not eat them all then someone I love will die.

- A group of us have to watch cows being killed; there is nothing we can do to stop the carnage.

- Staying in a hotel where I am forced to eat disgusting food combinations such as pickled onions and chocolate custard.

Dreams can be helpful in analysing exactly what it is that you are concerned about in your waking life. They often display your subconscious thoughts and give an indication of underlying issues which you might not yet feel able to accept. Although I was dangerously ill with anorexia, I never admitted to myself that I could die as a result. However, my dreams were filled with death, for which I was always responsible.

- My best friend is in hospital. She is dying and is covered in tubes but there is nothing I can do to help her. I just have to watch her die.

- I see a man sitting in a boat. It begins to rock and he falls overboard. I try and rescue him but I am too late and he drowns.

- I am following a car which skids, flips onto its side and then explodes. I try to save the people inside but there is nothing I can do. I have to watch them die knowing that it is my fault.

- I have to plug myself into a computer to recharge myself or else I will die. I know that I am running out of time but I can not find the computer.

I often had dreams in which groups of people pointed and laughed at me or where others said that they hated me.

- I am having a meal at a restaurant. Everyone has a normal amount except for me and so people start to point and laugh.

- I am in hospital and no one comes to visit me because they all hate me.

- I am walking home barefoot because I have lost my shoes and everyone is laughing and pointing at me.

- I am in a restaurant with my parents. My mother makes another nasty comment about how useless I am with food. I can not take this any longer and walk out. However, I begin to feel guilty and decide to return. As I turn to walk back into the room, I can hear her telling everyone what a stupid and horrible person I am.

Your dreams and nightmares may seem like an insignificant jumble at first, but if you keep recording them, a pattern will gradually start to emerge. As you make progress with your recovery, you may also see a change in your dreams.

I have noticed that I am no longer at fault all the time or the victim of everyone else's anger. Instead, I have become far more assertive in my dreams and have even shouted back at some of the people who have hurt me throughout my life.

Chapter 10

How to Stop Dangerous Behaviours

There are a number of behaviours which are linked to eating disorders that can be extremely detrimental to a sufferer's health. The major ones are bingeing, vomiting, laxative and diuretic abuse, overexercising and self-harm. This chapter will show different ways that these behaviours can be stopped. It can also be helpful to use some of the other techniques already discussed, such as CBT, and relaxation techniques as additional support if you are initially having a difficult time. This chapter works best if you read just the sections which correspond to your own particular behaviours.

How to stop bingeing

We currently live in a society where food is extremely plentiful and products such as fast food, sweets and fatty snacks are very cheap. These products are high in fat and sugar, which means that they have an attractive taste and frequently produce an instant euphoric high. These products are known as comfort foods and they are frequently eaten in large quantities as part of a binge.

Bingeing can occur for several reasons, both physical and emotional. Each reason requires a different treatment.

Physical reasons

Bingeing can take place simply because a person is feeling intensely hungry. Hunger plays a key role in the human body – in its extreme form, it forces the mind to focus on nothing but food and how it can be attained. This feeling will continue until food is consumed and the body is satisfied.

This means that anorexia or bulimia sufferers will be confronted by severe feelings of hunger when they diet strictly. Anorexia sufferers often force themselves to ignore the hunger pangs through sheer force of will, although they cannot stop their minds from concentrating on thoughts of food.

Bulimia sufferers frequently say that they wish they had more control since they feel weak for giving in to the hunger pangs and starting to binge. Some sufferers will fast for days and then feel so hungry that they can eat over 30,000 calories in a single sitting. Once they have binged, they then feel instantly guilty, which leads them to vomit, purge using laxatives, or both. As a result, sufferers begin fasting again, which, in turn, eventually triggers another binge and a dangerous cycle of behaviour is established.

The first step in controlling this behaviour is to stop the intense physical cravings which lead to the binges. This can be achieved in the following way.

- *Eating regular meals.* This is very important since it is the feelings of intense hunger which usually trigger binges. Make sure that you are eating the correct number of calories for your age and gender. For example, a woman in her twenties requires approximately 1950 calories per day and men of the same age need approximately 2400.

- *Avoid further negative behaviour.* If you do binge then make sure that you do not use any negative methods to try and compensate for this. Avoid vomiting, taking laxatives, overexercising or fasting, as any one of these will only make the situation far worse.

- *Continue regular eating.* If you have binged, continue to eat your agreed diet plan – if you try to compensate by skipping a meal then you are likely to trigger a binge/fast cycle.

- *Accept that periods can lead to cravings.* Female sufferers need to understand that they are likely to crave comfort foods such as chocolate during their monthly periods. Incorporate these foods into your daily eating plan so that you do not feel deprived and/or turn to bingeing to satisfy your cravings.

- *Avoid alcohol or recreational drugs.* These can both increase your appetite and may trigger a binge.

- *Include all food groups in your diet.* This includes normal quantities of your binge foods (such as chocolate or savoury snacks). If you are able to educate your mind into accepting that these foods are permitted in your daily diet, you are less likely to binge on them in secret.

- *Take extra exercise into account.* If you are doing any additional exercising then compensate for this by eating something extra. Do not allow yourself to get too hungry.

- *Plan in advance.* If you know that circumstances will cause you to miss a meal, make plans in advance to have a snack with you.

Emotional reasons

Bingeing does not only take place as a response to feeling physically hungry. It is often used by sufferers as a way of filling an emotional void or burying difficult feelings. Bingeing may occur if a person is feeling lonely, sad, hurt, angry, disappointed or anxious. If you can solve your problems in a healthy way then there will not be a need to turn to food as an escape.

Look instead at the alternative methods of dealing with emotions and try CBT, anger management or anxiety management. All of these therapies can make you feel emotionally better without resorting to overeating.

Practical steps to help you stop bingeing

- *Keep a diary of your binges.* Record everything in this. How did you feel before, during and after the binge? What caused you to binge? What did you eat? How long did the binge last? The more information you can include the better since you will gradually be able to see a pattern emerging. You can then learn what it is that triggers your binges and which are your most vulnerable times.

- *Plan alternative activities.* Once you have identified when you are most likely to binge, work out different activities for this particular period. Bingeing can often occur simply because the sufferer is feeling bored. Take up new hobbies and fill your free time with more exciting events.

- *Try to avoid being alone if this causes binges.* If you never binge when there are other people around, try to ensure that you have company during your most vulnerable times.

- *Ask for help.* If you are struggling, call a friend or go out for a walk to meet someone. Even window shopping or a trip to the local park can be a distraction which allows the need for a binge to pass.

- *Avoid food shopping.* Sufferers often choose binge foods when they are buying their weekly shopping on their own. Try asking a friend to go with you if this is likely to help. Stick rigidly to a pre-written list and avoid the aisles which feel too tempting, such as cakes or snacks.

- *Work on reducing the number of binges.* Calculate how many times a week you usually binge and draw up a plan to reduce this number. If you binge six times in one week, make sure that the next week it is only five times, then four the following week and so on.

- *Do not be hard on yourself.* When you do binge, try learning from the setback rather than criticizing yourself harshly. Identify why it happened and then look for solutions that will stop you from repeating the behaviour.

- *Do not give up.* If you are finding it difficult to change, ask for extra support or try to make a smaller change instead. Sufferers are usually so desperate to lose their illnesses that they can attempt to change too much too quickly.

How to stop vomiting

Many of the practical steps that have just been mentioned concerning bingeing are also very helpful if you are trying to stop vomiting.

Sufferers often feel deeply ashamed of their behaviour and so try to keep it a secret from their family and friends. However, it is easier to fight the disorder if you have a supportive network around you. Choose people who will encourage you through the difficult patches and trust them with your secrets. If they care about you, they should be able to help. Explain to them that you do not expect them to be able to solve your problems but if they can offer a friendly ear, this alone can make a tremendous difference.

Eating disorder sufferers who vomit fall into one of two categories:

- people who vomit many times a day

- people who vomit a few times each week.

People who vomit many times a day

Sufferers who fall into this group will vomit after every meal and usually after snacks as well. Vomiting has become an addiction here since they can not bear the feeling of food in their stomach. They are often so used to vomiting that it has become a natural reflex action and they no longer even have to induce the process.

It is more difficult to give up vomiting when it has become a way of life, although this makes it even more vital to stop because it is so dangerous. I would strongly recommend that your first step is to see a doctor to ensure that there is no physical damage to your body.

You then need to accept that you will feel full at times. It is likely that you find the feeling of fullness difficult to cope with, which is why you vomit so frequently. Use your relaxation techniques to help yourself cope with any stress that may arise as a result.

Exercise 10.1

Diary-keeping

The following two methods of giving up this behaviour both involve keeping a diary to record how many times a day you vomit. Keep your diary for a week before you attempt to give up the behaviour as this will give you a clear indication of the frequency of your vomiting.

Method 1

This approach involves cutting down slowly on the number of times you vomit. If this is six times a day then make sure that your new target is five times a day. Keep at this level for a week and then cut down again on the number. As you begin to approach the lower numbers, you may feel more anxious and need to make your changes at a slower rate.

For example, when you are vomiting twice a day, it may prove too stressful to halve this to just once. Try instead to look at the situation from a weekly perspective. Twice a day = 14 times a week. Decide to vomit only 12 times the following week and continue cutting down this way until the behaviour has completely ended.

Method 2

Another way of breaking the pattern of vomiting after meals is to delay the process. Start by working out exactly how long after your meal you vomit. If this is five minutes then your aim is to extend this time period. Add an extra five minutes so that you now wait for ten minutes before vomiting.

These extra minutes are likely to cause you to feel stressed, so rely on the methods already discussed. Try to be around other people while you are waiting, to avoid the temptation to vomit earlier than intended.

Once you have managed to wait for ten minutes for a full week, it is then time to make another change. Again, add an additional five or ten minutes – the choice is yours since you are in control of your recovery. Keep lengthening this time period until you feel that you are able to cut out the vomiting altogether.

Remind yourself that it does not matter if your progress is slow – any progress is positive and will contribute to your full recovery.

People who vomit a few times each week

Sufferers in this group do not vomit immediately after a binge but often wait for a few hours. They will also occasionally binge without vomiting at all.

If you fall into this second category then (just like an occasional smoker) you have more control over your illness and can use this same control in a positive way to enable recovery. Start by working out exactly how many times a week you vomit. For example, if it is five times then you need to make sure that you reduce this to four the following week. Continue this pattern until you have eventually abandoned the behaviour entirely.

Use distraction techniques, relaxation exercises and CBT to calm yourself when you feel anxious and want to vomit. Talk to friends on the phone, watch a favourite programme, have a bubble bath or go for a gentle walk. Use any of these (or other) healthy and positive ways of distracting yourself and defusing tension when the urge arises and you will learn to beat this compulsion.

How to give up laxatives

Laxatives are strong medications and using them incorrectly is extremely danger-ous. Laxative abuse can cause serious medical complications and could even prove fatal.

It can be helpful for sufferers to understand that these medications do not aid weight loss because they can not prevent the absorption of calories. Laxatives affect the large intestine and by the time food reaches this area all of the calories have already been absorbed.

If you notice a drop in weight after you have used laxatives, this is purely the result of a loss of water weight. Once you eat or drink anything, the body will quickly re-absorb the lost water so as to prevent dehydration. You may actually find that your weight rises slightly due to water retention. Sufferers who do not understand this process often panic when they see their weight rise and take even more laxatives as a result. However, this water-based weight gain will stop once you give up taking the laxatives.

The taking of excessive quantities of this medication has a strong detrimental effect on the bowel. It gradually becomes 'lazy', relying entirely on the laxatives to keep it functioning. This leads to severe bouts of constipation, which often cause the sufferer to take even higher numbers of laxatives.

Are you taking too many laxatives?

Try answering the following questions.

- Do you regularly use laxatives?

- Do you take more than the recommended dose?

- Do you frequently experience stomach cramps and/or diarrhoea?

- Do you take laxatives when you feel that you have eaten too much food?

- Do you conceal your laxative use from others?

- Do you buy laxatives from different shops so as to avoid suspicion?

- Do you experience constipation when you do not take laxatives?

- Have you found that you often need to increase the number of laxatives you take to have the same effect?

If you have answered 'yes' to a number of these questions then it is likely that you are abusing laxatives and risk severely damaging your body.

It is very important to let your doctor know that you are giving up these medications since he or she will be able to determine exactly which method is best for you. Your doctor can also monitor your progress, in addition to offering practical help if you are struggling.

There are currently two key approaches to giving up laxatives, although Method 1 is generally favoured by the medical profession.

METHOD 1

This approach involves discontinuing all laxative abuse immediately in order to minimize the damage to your body. Make sure that you dispose of all the laxatives in your possession so that you do not feel tempted to use them again.

Gently increase your fibre intake by eating an increased amount of fruit and vegetables, as well as soluble fibre in the form of food such as porridge oats or oat bran. Do not be tempted to eat large quantities of wheat bran since this is an insoluble fibre which leaches calcium from the body as it passes through and can leave bones brittle. Also ensure that you drink a minimum of eight glasses of water a day (two litres) as this will help to prevent constipation.

If you find that you are suffering from constipation, talk with your doctor since he or she will be able to prescribe a mild medication (or bulking agent) which can increase the fibre level in your diet.

It is also important to watch for swelling around the ankles, knees or fingers because this can be a sign of water retention (or 'oedema'). This can potentially occur in the days immediately after laxative abuse has ceased. It can be distressing for sufferers since they assume that they are growing 'fat'. This is *not* the case, however. It is a natural response within the body and it will pass quickly so long as the sufferer does not begin taking laxatives again.

METHOD 2

This approach is likely to be more appealing for sufferers since it is a gentler method. However, it does entail taking very dangerous medications for a longer period of time, which means a greater potential risk to health.

This method allows sufferers to gradually cut down on the number of laxatives they take while increasing the amount of fibre in their diet. If you experience bloating caused by constipation, it is possible to use natural fibre supplements which can be purchased from a pharmacy. These are only an interim measure though, as it is important to obtain all the daily fibre you require from your regular diet.

Dried fruit, such as apricots, prunes and figs, is a natural laxative and some sufferers find it beneficial to add an extra prune or apricot to their diet every time they cut out another laxative. As with Method 1, it remains important to drink plenty of water each day and to focus on eating soluble fibre such as oat bran (rather than insoluble fibre such as wheat bran).

If you have been taking laxatives for a while, your intestine may be 'sluggish' and function poorly as a result. Start by incorporating cooked fruit and vegetables which have had their skins removed into your diet. Only when your intestine is functioning properly should you begin adding raw fruit and vegetables.

Remember that giving up laxatives is a permanent change in your life. Do not keep a stash of 'emergency' pills hidden in your home because you may be tempted to use them, which would restart the whole cycle again.

How to give up diuretics

Diuretics are medications that are used to excrete additional water from the body. They are often prescribed for people with high blood pressure and women may take them around the time of their monthly period when they are retaining water.

These pills are frequently used by eating disorder sufferers who mistakenly believe that they will assist weight loss. As with laxatives, diuretics are totally ineffective in this area since they only cause water to be lost from the body.

These medications are also dangerous since they can cause oedema, constipation, weakness, nausea, abdominal pain and heart irregularities. Diuretics affect the body's electrolyte balance, which can have extremely serious physical consequences.

Treatment for sufferers who want to stop taking diuretics is similar to those for people who abuse laxatives (either stopping immediately or reducing the intake gradually). It is also important to let your doctor know that you have been taking these medications.

If there are any other substances you are taking in an attempt to advance weight loss (such as diet pills or emetics) these should also be stopped using the methods previously outlined.

How to stop overexercising

The feelings of guilt caused by eating often result in sufferers trying to burn up any calories they have consumed. This means that they frequently exercise during any available spare moment. This is not a healthy situation since excessive exercise places an even greater strain on an already weakened physical state.

Both anorexia and bulimia sufferers are in danger of damaging their heart if they exercise vigorously. Overeaters who are normally sedentary may also endanger their health by suddenly engaging in high levels of exercise if they are not used to it.

If you are choosing recovery then it is vital to stop overexercising. Weight gain is even more difficult for anorexia sufferers if they continue to use up all of the calories ingested. It is important to let family and friends know if you are exercising secretly since they should be able to offer support and encouragement when you feel anxious.

If you are at a low weight, you should completely stop all exercising until your body is physically stronger. Try starting up a new hobby or use the time you would have spent exercising with friends instead. Keep your mind occupied and use CBT to help you work through any feelings of guilt you may encounter.

You may have been using exercise as an unhealthy way of blocking out any difficult or painful emotions that you were experiencing. Try instead to confront these difficult feelings. It may be that counselling or therapy could help you to deal with these in a positive way.

Remember that it is extremely dangerous to exercise if your body has no fuel. As you recover and start to include gentle exercises in your routine, it is vital that you eat extra food to compensate for the calories you burn up.

How to stop self-harming

Self-harm or self-inflicted violence (SIV) is the deliberate harming of your own body without any intention of committing suicide. It is often linked to eating disorders since quite a high percentage of sufferers do also inflict physical damage on themselves deliberately.

Although it may sound strange, self-harming is usually a way of attempting to cope in a crisis. It enables sufferers to continue their life by physically expressing their tensions and emotional pain. Some sufferers say that they actually feel more peaceful after they have cut themselves. Others say that their life has made them feel numb and cutting at least allows them to experience pain so that they feel alive again.

I found that I cut myself for two reasons:

- I was experiencing deep emotional pain from years of sustained family abuse. By cutting myself, I was trying to cover these feelings of hurt with a different physical pain.

- I felt that I was a bad person and was trying to punish myself. Whenever anyone was unhappy in my family, I felt that I had caused this and would injure myself as a punishment.

I felt guilty whenever I ate and was convinced that I did not actually deserve food. Even when I did eat, I often punished myself by cutting.

Saturday 29 March 1997

I cut myself deliberately today. I understand that it doesn't solve my problems but I just felt I had to do it. I was feeling so miserable. I'd managed to eat some extra food (I'd just been told that I had to or else I'd have to go back into hospital) and I was hating myself.

I couldn't stop calling myself a fat pig. I believed that if I cut myself, the physical pain might block out some of this mental torment. I also thought that I really deserved to hurt for being such a greedy cow. But it didn't take away any of the sadness and now I've got deep cuts that will be with me as scars for ever.

Not all eating disorder sufferers self-harm though. Look at the following description to see if you carry out this behaviour. Self-harming is defined by the following criteria:

- It is done to yourself.

- It is carried out by yourself.

- It is not a suicide attempt.

- It is intentional and carried out on purpose.

- It is physically violent and causes temporary damage to the body (it will heal within a few days but you may be left with scars).

Identifying your self-harm triggers

If you are a self-harmer then it is important to identify your triggers.

- Self-harm is often used as a way of coping with difficult emotions such as anger, fear, anxiety, depression or extreme tension.

- It can be a way of coping with a perceived loss, such as when a friend cancels a date. This can leave a person feeling isolated and abandoned. He or she self-harms as a means of blocking these painful feelings.

- Sufferers may feel numb and 'dead' inside. This can lead them to self-harm so as to feel 'alive' again. They believe that feeling pain is better than feeling nothing at all.

- Self-harm is often used by sufferers as a way of punishing themselves. They may experience guilt (despite not actually having done anything wrong) and self-harm assuages this feeling.

- It can be used as a way of feeling in control. Eating disorders often develop as a means of controlling your life and self-harm can be an extension of this.

Once you have identified exactly what it is that causes you to self-harm then you can begin to end this damaging pattern of behaviour. There are many different ways of stopping self-harming, some of which have already been covered. CBT, distraction techniques, relaxation exercises and anger management are all appropriate strategies that work well for sufferers.

Another method of treatment which has proved highly beneficial is problem-solving. The idea behind this strategy is that problems in your daily life often cause you to experience negative and unpleasant emotions. These issues can also trigger the physical symptoms of anxiety, panic attacks, headaches, insomnia and so on. People often focus on these physical symptoms and ignore the underlying problems which have triggered the whole episode.

If you can effectively deal with the problems in your life then you are far less likely to experience difficult physical and emotional feelings. If you are feeling calmer and are handling your problems well, self-harming will not be seen as the 'solution'.

Exercise 10.2

Problem-solving

List all of your problems

Begin by writing down all of the problems which are currently affecting your life. Do not focus just on food or weight issues but extend the list to include problems such as work, relationships, finance, friends, loneliness or even legal issues (such as a divorce).

Isolate one problem

When you first look at your completed list, it will probably feel quite intimidating. Try not to feel disheartened though because you are going to tackle the problems one at a time. Remember that progressing in baby steps works well for most sufferers. Identify which problem you would like to work on first. This is likely to be the problem which has been occupying your mind most often.

Set a target

It is now time to work out exactly what you want. How would your life change if you did not have this problem? What would be different? Would you socialize more as a result for example?

Your aim or target needs to be specific – if you keep it vague, such as 'I want to be happy,' it will be almost impossible to achieve. Even people who are content with their lives are not able to remain happy all the time.

Be specific and break down a general target into a number of smaller ones, such as 'I want to eat a bar of chocolate' or 'I want to make a phone call.' These were targets which I set for myself when I was recovering. Chocolate had become a 'forbidden' food which I had denied myself and I was afraid of making telephone calls.

Find solutions

Once you have isolated a specific problem, you then need to look for solutions. Write down any ideas which occur to you in relation to this problem. At this point, do not make any judgements about how realistic you feel they might be. The more ideas you can record, the easier it will be to choose the appropriate solution.

Pick your solution

Examine your list of ideas. Is there one which strikes you as the most effective? It may be that a number of these ideas could work well. If this is the case, then place them in order with your preferred option at the top of the list.

Plan your approach

Once the solution has been chosen, you will need to draw up a plan to help enable you to carry it out. List all the steps you will need to take if you are to be successful with this new approach.

Take action

Now it is time to put your plan into action. Carefully follow the steps you previously drew up and see what happens.

Examine the results

Take stock and see if you have reached your chosen target. Did your solution work? Did any complications arise which you did not expect? Do you need to go back and pick another approach? If you were successful and you solved your problem then move on to the next one down on your original list.

Self-harm often feels like a temporary solution to your problems but it can never change them for the better. By using this problem-solving method, you can identify which situations are causing you to feel so low. Through working on a plan, you can actually solve the problem without resorting to self-harm.

Many sufferers who have tried this therapeutic approach have said that it left them feeling far more positive in general and the urge to self-harm had passed. Simply making a plan can often lift people's mood and allows to see that their situation is not hopeless. They may have previously felt impotent and unable to alter anything in their life. This method gives them some focus and a goal to work towards.

Chapter 11

Anger Management

Anger is a normal, healthy human emotion which we all experience frequently. Like other emotions, it causes physiological and biological changes to the body. When you become angry, your heart rate and blood pressure rise, as well as your hormone and adrenaline levels.

Often, eating disorder sufferers say that they do not experience certain emotions, including anger. This is not true though since everyone feels anger from time to time. However, many sufferers will cover this emotion with their illness.

For example, bulimia sufferers use bingeing and vomiting as a way of concealing their true emotions. If they feel angry they will start to eat, although their mind is then overtaken by the physical urge to binge and then eventually vomit. This becomes their sole focus and the underlying anger is soon forgotten.

It is vital that eating disorder sufferers learn how to express their anger in a positive way. It is important that they do not harm themselves and also that they do not take out any destructive behaviour on the people around them.

There are three common ways that people deal with their anger.

1. *Expressing it.* This means that they display their anger openly towards one or more people. It is important to try and do this in a controlled way.

2. *Suppressing it.* This means that people 'sit' on their anger and this is a dangerous tactic often used by sufferers. The danger here is that they will be unable to cope with the levels of anger that they experience and are more likely to turn it inwards upon themselves (such as by self-harming or overexercising).#

3. *Calming it.* This means that you control both your internal feelings of rage as well as the external signs that you are angry. This includes methods such as deep breathing and relaxation techniques to slow your heartbeat.

Expressing anger

The instinctive way to express anger is to behave in an aggressive manner. This is a natural instinct whenever we feel threatened or attacked. However, it is frequently an inappropriate response which causes more problems than it solves.

The healthiest way to express anger is in an assertive, non-aggressive manner. This means that you clearly show others what your needs are in a calm, reasonable way without hurting them. It is important to understand, though, that being assertive does not mean behaving in a pushy or demanding way. Often, when people get angry, they are confident that their feelings are correct and that they are fully justified.

Calmly examine what it is that is making you angry. Is it fair? Should you be expressing your feelings in this way? How would you feel if the situation was reversed and someone was approaching you in this way? Is this a constructive way to express how you feel?

If you have assessed the problem and still believe that it is justified for you to feel angry, you then need to make a plan. Work out how you can calmly and reasonably talk through your issues.

Apart from the damaging effects of the anger on yourself, people are far more likely to listen to you seriously if you approach them in a calmer way. Sometimes it can help to get your thoughts down on paper in the form of a letter (you do not need to send this to anyone).

Try to be non-judgemental. Avoid beginning sentences with phrases such as: 'You have made me feel useless.' Instead, try to phrase things in such a way that you will not immediately make the other person defensive. For example, 'This situation has caused my confidence to drop and I am not feeling very good about myself at the moment.'

It is also important to ask questions in order to establish the truth. Mistakes are often made which are unintentional but might be seen as deliberate by someone else. One example in an office situation might go as follows.

> At 11.45 am, Cathy goes to the fridge and uses the last of the milk
> in her coffee. She knows that her lunch break is due in 15 minutes

and she plans to buy a new pint for everyone. At 11.55 am, her boss calls her in for an urgent meeting, which causes her to miss her lunch and not return to her desk until 3.00 pm. By this time though, everyone is giving her angry glares for using the last of the milk and failing to replace it.

It is likely that any incidents which anger you are of much greater significance than this small example but it does illustrate how important it is to know your facts before judging and then confronting someone.

Suppressing anger

Suppressing anger is another method of dealing with difficult emotions. Once suppressed, anger can then be changed into more positive and constructive behaviour. However, there is the danger that if you continually suppress your anger and allow it no outward expression, it can be turned inwards instead. It then becomes destructive and can result in eating disorders, self-harm, depression, high blood pressure and many other physical conditions.

Unexpressed anger can also be used as a weapon and may result in passive aggression. This is where a person never directly confronts a problem but tries to hurt people indirectly without telling them why.

For example, a young man in his late twenties who wrote to me was full of anger and extremely unhappy as a result. He believed that nobody understood him and he felt constantly undermined by his partner, his children, work colleagues and friends. As a result, he used passive aggression on a daily basis to try and annoy others. The more upset or angry they became, the happier he was. Watching other people suffer in the way that he believed himself to be suffering helped to release his tensions.

He would never directly admit to feelings of anger, although his actual behaviour displayed intense inner rage. A therapist later pointed out to him just how angry he really was at those around him. The bubble immediately burst and he no longer felt able to play tricks or try and aggravate those around him to defuse his anger. As a result, he learnt to accept his rage and began to deal with it constructively.

Calming anger

The third method of dealing with anger is calming both your outward behaviour and your internal reactions. By consciously breathing deeply and lowering your heart rate, you will begin to feel calmer. I often use CBT to help me if I am feeling angry. Positive self-talk can help defuse a situation and logic can disarm anger. The aim of anger management is to reduce the emotional and physical responses that occur whenever you feel angry.

Eating disorder sufferers frequently experience intense anger, such as when they feel that they are being forced to eat against their will. This can lead to destructive behaviour both towards themselves (self-harm, starvation, over-exercise, laxative abuse and so on) and others (such as throwing plates of food or shouting and screaming). It is important to learn ways of managing your own anger.

Remember that the world is not 'out to get you'. If anorexia sufferers feel as though people are forcing food on to them, this is likely to be because they are concerned about how thin they have become. Try not to view everyone as the enemy but instead as a member of a potential support network.

At the time of my own eating disorder, I did not believe that I even experienced anger at all. Of course this was not the case and I felt very angry much of the time. However, instead of expressing it, I turned it inwards upon myself, which defused it for a while. Eating disorders are angry illnesses. Sufferers often feel intense rage if they eat more than they feel they are permitted and will punish themselves harshly as a result. It is this kind of anger which needs to be managed.

In the past, many psychologists believed it was important for patients to give voice to all their angry feelings. However, it is now often felt that this approach can encourage aggression and may not help the situation. Anger is now often viewed as a frustrated desire or blocked wish. The more recent attitude is that helping patients to manage their feelings towards this blocked wish is the key to treatment.

Be honest with yourself. Are you feeling angry for a justified reason or is it perhaps that things are not going your way at the moment?

It is important to discover exactly what it is that causes you to feel angry. In the following exercise, list all the times you have felt angry in the last day and then the reasons why. It is essential to list any that do not relate directly to your eating disorder as well.

The following are a couple of examples from my own life, to give you an idea of what to list.

- The television broke down today and now I will have to get in a repair man.

- I spilt coffee on the bed and had to change and wash all of the bed covers.

Now list your own events:

Exercise 11.1

Reasons I felt angry today

_____

_____

_____

_____

_____

_____

When you have finished listing all of the incidents, take a look at the completed list. Is there a common thread? Can you identify what it is that triggers your anger? Once you begin to see a pattern then you can develop ways of dealing with the anger.

The following are some suggestions to help you cope.

- *Learn relaxation techniques.* Popular techniques include deep breathing exercises or using visual imagery. Some people find it beneficial to repeat a phrase to themselves in times of stress, such as 'take it easy' whilst calming their breathing. Others visualize a pleasant and relaxing experience or memory from their past. Certain non-strenuous stretching exercises can also relax and calm tense muscles.

- *CBT.* Altering your thinking can help you to change the way you feel. When people are angry, their thought processes become exaggerated and dramatic. For example, if you think, 'It's the end of the world. Everything is ruined. I am so angry,' try replacing these beliefs with

'This is just a small problem which I can handle. There's no point getting upset about it.'

Try not to use words which feel permanent like 'always' and 'never' (such as 'I am always such a failure' or 'You never get it right') when you are angry since they are rarely accurate and are only likely to escalate the situation. Using terms like these causes others to feel defensive and make it harder to resolve a problem.

Also try to use logic to fight your rage because even when it is justified, anger can quickly become irrational. People who are quick to anger often have a demanding nature and it can help to pause and examine the wider picture, including how right we really are and what are unrealistic demands on others. Should a husband expect his wife always to cook the dinner? Should a child always have sweets when he or she is taken shopping?

Often, a demanding nature has its roots in childhood. Some parents feel that they should try to give their children everything and this can lead to problems of expectation in later life.

- *Use humour.* It may seem impossible at times to look at the lighter side of a situation when you are feeling angry but the rewards can be immense. Watching a favourite comedy programme, remembering a funny incident or just taking yourself less seriously can help to bring things back into perspective. It is extremely difficult to keep hold of your anger and sense of injustice when you are laughing.

  Try to take your problems less seriously. In the 1939 film version of 'Goodbye Mr Chips', Mr Chippings (a teacher at a boy's school) said: 'Give a boy a sense of humour and a sense of proportion and he'll stand up to anything.'

- *Talk more.* Anger often occurs because of simple misunderstandings. Talk through your problems with other people and you will often find a new perspective on the situation and learn that you have been jumping to incorrect conclusions.

- *Calmly examine your situation.* Another potential source of anger is the thought that certain daily problems are insoluble, such as rush-hour traffic or other people's rudeness. The Roman philosopher Seneca compared anger with a dog that is tied to a cart which is rolling downhill. The dog can pull and strain at the lead, trying in vain to escape the cart but this will only cause greater distress. The alternative is to accept the situation and move peacefully with the cart, even enjoying the journey. Some problems do not have simple solutions but our attitudes to them can change the way in which we experience them. These problems will still be there whether we are angry or calm, so why not try and be calm?

Exercise 11.2

Anger management

Below is a list of situations which can potentially make an eating disorder sufferer angry. Try and find a positive solution for each one, using some of the techniques discussed.

Problem 1

You are out with friends and they are pushing you to have a dessert. You feel angry and close to tears. You want to knock the sweet trolley over but at the same time you would also really like to have the dessert.

Possible solution

Use deep breathing to calm yourself down and then ask if you could share a dessert with one of your friends. Explain to them that you just couldn't manage one by yourself. Trust and honesty is very important between friends.

Problem 2

You have an appointment to see a doctor. You feel upset that people are interfering in your life when you just want to be left alone.

Possible solution

Be honest with yourself. Do you really want to be alone? I know that I felt isolated and scared when I was anorexic and, although help seemed threatening, it also felt very reassuring. Is your anger here really just fear in disguise? Perhaps it is time to accept help from professionals who care.

Problem 3

The supermarket has run out of your usual food. You do not know what to do and feel angry with the shop.

Possible solution

Do you need to eat exactly the same food every day? Change can be a positive thing and it can also help to break some of your rules. It is likely that the store has another interesting item which has roughly the same calories.

Problem 4

Your disordered eating leads to mood swings and today you feel upset with everyone around you. It makes you want to simply hide away.

Possible solution

Eating regular meals will help to regulate your moods. Perhaps it is time to consider following a structured eating plan. Remember that you can begin slowly and at your own chosen pace.

Try this exercise using some of your own experiences and work out calm and positive solutions to each one.

Problem

_____

_____

Possible solution

_____

_____

_____

Problem

_____

_____

Possible solution

_____

_____

_____

Problem

_____

_____

Possible solution

_____

_____

Exercise 11.3

Anger feelings

Learn to be honest about your feelings and admit to when you are feeling angry. Sufferers frequently feel threatened by people who offer support since they are not yet ready to give up their eating disorders. This can lead sufferers to make defensive remarks to deflect other people and prevent them from getting close. The following are some examples.

You say: 'You don't understand what it's like to have an eating disorder. How can you possibly help me?'

You mean: 'I am frightened of losing control and allowing other people to have a strong influence in my life.'

You say: 'No one ever actually recovers from an eating disorder despite what they might say.'

You mean: 'If I refuse to believe that recovery is even possible then I have a permanent excuse not to try.'

Have you had any thoughts like these?

Try and list some angry thoughts or remarks you have made and then work out what the underlying reason might have been.

You say:

_____

_____

You mean:

_____

_____

You say:

_____

_____

You mean:

_____

_____

You say:

_____

_____

You mean:

_____

_____

When you are struggling with anger and feel hopeless, see if you can hold on to more positive thoughts which improve your mood. If you allow them to, these thoughts will eventually allow the anger to subside and leave you in a calmer frame of mind.

Anger is often rooted in fear. When people are afraid they usually feel powerless and out of control. Anger can redress this balance and leave people feeling as though they are more powerful. This is a false belief though.

If you are afraid of a situation, the most positive approach is to deal with it directly rather than defending your position with anger. Try asking for some help and talk about your fears. Putting your anger and pride to one side allows you to reach out for some much-needed help.

Chapter 12

Anxiety Management

Anxiety is often referred to as a single entity but it can be broken down into three separate components.

1. *Physical feelings*. These are the feelings listed in Table 12.1 – sweating, rapid heartbeat, churning stomach, breathlessness, shakiness and so on.

2. *The 'fight or flight' action*. This refers to the way a person behaves during an anxiety attack.

3. *Internal thoughts*. This includes your thoughts and beliefs whenever an anxiety attack occurs. It also involves your fears and ideas about the consequences of facing a frightening situation.

What is anxiety?

Anxiety is the body's natural response to a potentially threatening situation. This reaction is often referred to as the 'fight or flight' response, and prepares a person to take action in order to survive. It forces the body to work harder and faster so as to escape the perceived danger. For example, if you are crossing the road and notice a car speeding towards you, it is your anxiety which helps you to react fast enough to move out of its way.

When a person senses a danger, the brain reacts by sending a message to the adrenal glands. This causes adrenal glands to release adrenaline into the bloodstream, which is then carried around the body. When it reaches the heart, lungs and muscles, it effects changes which help the person to either escape or retaliate.

Table 12.1 Anxiety attacks

What happens to the body	How this makes you feel
The initial visual sharpening (which causes you to notice the danger) fades	Vision is disturbed and blurry
Body fluid such as saliva is redirected into the bloodstream	This results in a dry mouth, which leads to difficulty swallowing and often trouble speaking as well
The air passages widen to allow more oxygen to pass into the lungs, allowing them to work harder	This redirection of oxygen causes breathlessness
The heart begins to beat harder so that more oxygen and energy passes to the muscles	You experience a racing heartbeat, which can feel like palpitations
The liver releases extra stored energy	If this energy is not used for 'flight or fight', it can lead to an uncomfortable restlessness
The intestines and stomach shut down; blood and energy are diverted to the muscles	The stomach feels strange; people often describe this as a feeling of 'butterflies' or a 'knotted tightness'
The skin becomes damp from sweat, which is produced in an attempt to cool the muscles	Hot flushes and sweating
Blood is diverted from the skin to the working muscles	Your face becomes pale
Muscles are now tense, in preparation for working harder	Tension is felt in the muscles; aches and pains are experienced, as well as frequent shaking
Calcium is discharged from the working muscles	This results in 'pins and needles'

Table 12.1 shows just how many functions come into play when a person becomes anxious. They are all vital should there be genuine danger. However, people will often feel threatened when there is not actually anything to run from or fight. This can lead to them feeling very physically uncomfortable. Adrenaline has been released so that action can be taken, even though it is not needed.

What frequently happens next is that people run away from the awkward situation or imagined threat, which causes them to feel relieved. This teaches them that running away makes them feels better and so a pattern of behaviour begins to develop. In the future, whenever a difficult situation arises, they run away instead of facing it. This is known as 'avoidance behaviour'.

If they had remained in the situation and felt uncomfortable, however, they would have discovered that as the adrenaline dissipated in the body, they would have begun to feel better.

Unfortunately, our anxieties are usually compounded by negative thoughts, such as:

> This is terrible. I feel so bad.

> This is never going to end. I've got to get away.

> People are looking at me. They think I'm stupid.

> I want to be somewhere else.

These negative thoughts cause sufferers to feel even more frightened, which leads to the release of extra adrenaline. This in turn makes them feel intensely uncomfortable and more desperate to escape.

Many eating disorder sufferers have anxiety attacks when faced with more food than they feel they should eat or when eating in public. This results in a rising level of panic and sufferers experience the full range of physical sensations outlined above. Instead of coping with these feelings, they try to avoid situations where they are not in control of their food intake. This causes the anxiety to develop further, ultimately leaving the sufferer feeling unable to cope.

It is very helpful to identify your fears and phobias before you are able to tackle them. Try listing them, in Exercise 12.1. Bear each item of your list in mind as you read the rest of this chapter and see how the techniques to relieve anxiety would apply to each fear.

Five important facts to remember

1. Anxiety is a normal physical reaction.
2. Anxiety is a useful function which can help to deal with a dangerous situation.
3. Unpleasant and uncomfortable physical sensations are due to the anxiety.
4. Negative thoughts will make the anxiety worse.
5. Anxiety is not dangerous and is not harmful.

Exercise 12.1

My anxiety list

List the situations which make you feel the most anxious. It is likely that many of these will be food-related but you may also have a social anxiety (such as a fear of talking to strangers at parties) or a particular phobia (such as the dark).

_____

_____

_____

_____

_____

_____

_____

_____

_____

_____

How to improve your life by controlling your anxiety

- *Learn to understand the process of anxiety.* As described earlier, anxiety can form a vicious circle. The more anxious you feel, the more physical symptoms you will experience, resulting in yet more anxiety. Break the cycle by accepting what has happened. Complaining or panicking will not prevent an anxiety attack once it has started. Accept it by taking a deep breath, dropping your shoulders and understanding that you are safe.

- *Learn new techniques for controlling your anxiety.* The most important action to take here is to relax. Notice that when an anxiety attack occurs, your breathing will be fast and shallow. Aim to make it both slow and deep. The deeper your breathing, the calmer you will feel. Learn some of the relaxation and controlled breathing exercises described later in this chapter.

Mental symptoms (constant worrying and negative thinking) can be reduced through using CBT. Identify the negative thoughts which are causing you to worry and then challenge them with positive responses.

You can also use exposure therapy to make behavioural changes. By acknowledging the situations which cause you anxiety, you can gradually face these fears step by step. As the exposure process continues, your anxiety levels will diminish over time.

- *Lifestyle can cause the most stress.* Uncomfortable relationships which lack honesty, a demanding job which is too pressurized, or too many commitments can lead to increased levels of stress and anxiety. It is important to become more assertive in your life and take back the control. You could learn how to manage your time more effectively, start to break negative habits or discover some new coping skills.

- *Try to be honest about your real anxiety levels.* People often pretend that they are fine because they do not want to appear weak or incompetent. However, if you trust others with your fears, they may be able to help you. They might even have similar fears themselves which they were keeping hidden. If this is the case, you can provide support and help for one another.

- *Learn to be patient.* The worst reaction to an anxiety attack is to panic since this results in the release of more adrenaline. If you can patiently wait as the adrenaline is used up, the anxious feelings will gradually subside.

Try to cope during the most difficult moments by concentrating on something outside of yourself. Study your surroundings in careful detail, for example. This distraction technique is not 'running away' from your feelings – in fact it is the opposite (it is staying in the moment and actually being aware of where you are rather than trying to escape it). By not giving the anxiety attack the attention that normally fuels it, you will allow it to pass.

The fear of the symptoms of fear is often referred to as 'the second fear'. First fears are usually life-saving and essential, as with our earlier example of avoiding a speeding car. However, second fears are the ones which become most predominant in the lives of anxiety sufferers. They are ultimately useless and debilitating, and need to be fought with logic.

- *Gently resume your life.* When the anxious feelings have passed, continue with what you were doing in a slow, calm and gentle manner. Take your time and remind yourself that there is no rush. Set yourself an achievable target (such as making a cup of tea or having a conversation with a friend) and only when you have achieved this should you set yourself another one. This will help you to reach your ultimate target by degrees.

Anxiety attacks are usually brought on when a sufferer tries to do too much too soon. It may take longer to reach your goal with baby steps but it will allow you to change your life permanently.

Relaxation exercises

The following exercises are all helpful during an anxiety attack. They teach sufferers to calm their breathing and relax muscles, as well as focusing the mind away from their anxieties. All of these exercises were taught to me when I was in hospital and I found them helpful.

Exercise 12.2

Feather exercise

Imagine that a feather is stuck to the end of your nose. Close your eyes and really *see* it there. Try to breathe very slowly and gently, so that you do not dislodge the feather.

When you feel that you have mastered this then you can incorporate counting. In your head, count from one to five as you release one breath without dislodging the feather. Do this three times. Then change to counting from one to five on the in breath. Do this three times as well.

Do not be hard on yourself if you find the exercise difficult – it becomes easier with practice.

Exercise 12.3

Abdominal breathing

Try to draw breath low down in your lungs. Place your hands on your abdomen. You should feel your abdomen rise (as you breathe in) and fall (as you breathe out). Concentrate on this for a few breaths. It may feel quite difficult at first because this is the reverse of what your diaphragm is used to doing. Once you have perfected this technique, allow yourself to enjoy it since it can leave you with a calm, serene feeling that is very helpful during periods of anxiety.

Exercise 12.4

Fast relaxation technique

This exercise incorporates general relaxation with gentle breathing and a loosening of muscles. Stand in a comfortable position with your weight evenly distributed between each foot. As you breathe, slowly release the tension in your forehead and jaw by relaxing these muscles. Move your arms, neck and shoulders gently and then continue by letting go of the tension from your stomach, back and legs. Keep breathing calmly and return to what you were doing before the anxiety attack occurred.

Exercise 12.5

Slow relaxation technique

Sit in a comfortable position, ensuring that your muscles are doing as little as possible. Take a few deep breaths and then begin to talk yourself through the exercise. Starting at your feet, gently clench and relax these muscles. As you relax them, tell that part of your body to go to sleep. Gradually work your way around your entire body, finishing by tensing and then relaxing your facial muscles.

Exercise 12.6

Listening exercise

Sufferers tend to be plagued by a stream of distressing and negative thoughts. To break these thought patterns, try closing your eyes and listening. Concentrate on each sound you hear around you. Focus all your attention on the task and continue working at this until you feel a little calmer.

Exercise 12.7

Repetition exercise

The repetition of useful phrases can also help with recovery. If you are beginning to feel panic-stricken, start repeating the following phrase to yourself – 'Anxiety is normal and these feelings cannot harm me.' Keep saying the phrase to yourself, each time emphasizing a different word in the sentence. Repetition of this kind of reassuring statement can aid relaxation.

Exercise 12.8

Distraction techniques

Distraction techniques draw your mind away from the focus of your anxiety. They stop you from filling your head with negative thoughts which can only exacerbate the problem. Try using the following distraction techniques.

Mental games

Puzzles such as sudoku, crosswords or word games in general are popular entertainment and can be good distractions. If you do not like these, try reciting a poem, singing a song, counting backwards, mental arithmetic or anything which will occupy your mind. All of these approaches help shift the focus from your internal problems to external interests.

Physical activity

Keeping yourself physically active can be helpful if you are feeling anxious. This can be a simple task, such as washing up after a meal or walking your dog. Combine this activity with a mental game such as counting backwards as an added distraction. If you are at a low weight, however, it may be dangerous to be physically active so check with your doctor first.

Exercise 12.9

Noticing

Sit down at a window or with something visually interesting in front of you. Close your eyes and adjust your posture. Imagine that an invisible string is attached to the top of your head. As you think of it being gently pulled, your spine and back should gradually straighten. Take a few deep breaths and then open your eyes.

Start to look around and say what it is that you see. Describe the colours, shapes, sounds, movements, smells and the feel of everything around you. If you are observing a treasured object, remind yourself why it is special. Recapture the positive feelings which this object has brought to you over the years. Try to continue this exercise until you are feeling calmer.

Conclusion

All of these exercises can be highly beneficial when you are experiencing anxiety. Eating disorder sufferers usually feel at their most anxious before, during and after meals. Practise using these exercises during times like these. Remember to persevere if they seem difficult at first. Eating disorders thrive on anxiety and your recovery will progress if you can learn to cope with such stressful periods. Without the feelings of anxiety and fear concerning food, there really is no eating disorder at all so these are very positive techniques to master.

Chapter 13

Assertiveness Training

As human beings, we all have needs and it is important that these are met in a healthy way in our daily lives. When people suffer from an eating disorder, their basic needs are no longer being met. This chapter aims to help you identify your own specific needs and teach you how to fulfil them.

Identifying your needs

The first step is to identify your actual needs. These should be healthy needs which are good for your mind and body. For example, anorexia suffers should not define a need as 'I need to continue losing weight' since this is a symptom of their illness. A healthy need would be 'I need to gain weight to the correct level for my height so that I can lead an active and fulfilling life.'

When I was in hospital, one of the first exercises that we completed was to list our own personal needs. My finished list is given below.

List of needs

1. I need reassurance that I am not always at fault. At the moment, I feel that I am to blame for everything which goes wrong and that makes me a failure.

2. I need to feel loved. I do not like myself at all and do not believe that anyone else could (or does).

3. I need to stop keeping all my worries to myself. I am not a nuisance if I ask people for advice.

4. I need to learn that it is OK to ask for help. People feel honoured if you turn to them in a time of need.

5. I need to learn how to cope with feeling fearful.

6. I need to stop trying to please everyone all of the time.

7. I need to consider my own well being and look after myself in a healthy way. This is not selfish.

8. I need to regain some self-esteem and confidence.

9. I need to learn to like myself.

Now try making a list of your own needs.

Exercise 13.1

My needs

_____

_____

_____

_____

_____

_____

_____

_____

_____

_____

Now that you have a list of your own emotional needs, it is time to learn how to fulfil them assertively.

Behaving in an assertive manner means that people stand up for their personal rights. They express their thoughts, beliefs and feelings in an open, direct and honest way that shows respect for the rights of others. They act in a responsible manner, which means that they do not feel anxiety or guilt. They recognize what they need from others and ask for this in a calm and direct way.

This does not mean that they will always get what they request, but their reaction to a refusal is equally important. They naturally feel disappointed or even sad but they do not lose confidence or feel that their self-esteem has been damaged as a result. This healthy reaction shows that their self-esteem is not based on the approval of others – it comes from within themselves. Being assertive means that they treat others in the way that they would like to be treated in return.

The aim of assertiveness behaviour is to communicate clearly with other adults. It shows that you will not allow others to take advantage of you and that you are a reasonable person who does not attack anyone who puts forward an opposing view.

Some people tend to confuse assertiveness with pushiness and aggression. If you are angry and shouting then you are no longer behaving in an assertive manner – you have actually just lost control. Table 13.1 illustrates the differences between assertiveness and aggression.

There are many benefits of learning to behave assertively. The more you stand up for yourself in a reasonable and respectful way, the higher your self-esteem will grow. People who do not express themselves assertively usually experience anxiety problems. Try looking at the following questions – do they describe you?

- Do you avoid expressing your own feelings?

- Do you often feel angry with others but suppress this feeling?

- Are you afraid of conflict and so pretend to be fine even if another person has upset you?

If you never tell others when you are upset, resentment will quickly build up. Expressing yourself directly and honestly will actually help to avoid conflict.

Learning assertive behaviour

The first step to being assertive is learning what behaviour actually entails. People who are naturally assertive probably do not even realize that they are behaving in this way. However, it can be useful to observe them since there are some universally recognizable traits, which are worth learning from.

Table 13.1 Assertive or aggressive?

Assertive behaviour	Aggressive behaviour
Direct eye contact	Trying to intimidate by staring intensely
Using a firm relaxed voice with smiles in between sentences	Using a loud harsh voice, often shouting and being demanding
Using terms which explain the situation, such as 'I want' or 'I don't think'	Using judgemental phrases, such as 'You are wrong' or 'You make me feel…', often spoken very fast
An open stance that is relaxed	A closed, cross-armed stance; movements such as finger-pointing and fist-clenching are common
The voice has a clear tone of sincerity	The tone is sarcastic and cold while the words themselves are often cruel
Co-operative phrases are used to show that negotiation is possible	There is no possibility of resolving the problem because pride is involved and they will not back down
The aim is that both parties are satisfied with the outcome	The aim is that one party has their say, leaving the other feeling upset and hurt
Facial features are steady throughout, with a relaxed jaw	There is frequent scowling and sneering, with a tense jawline

Dos

- Make statements which are short, distinct and reflect your feelings, such as: 'I like', 'I feel', 'I think', 'I want' and so on.

- If you are making a suggestion, avoid using judgemental terms such as 'should' or 'ought to'. Try to keep the question or comment open instead, so that the other person feels able to give his or her opinion. For example: 'Would you like me to pick you up from the station?' rather than: 'You shouldn't walk home alone – I'll pick you up from the station.' The second comment is too controlling and leaves no room for choice.

- Do not give an opinion as a statement of fact. Make sure that it is clear that this is your opinion by using phrases such as 'I often find …'. Offer advice or encouragement but do not try to force people to adopt your way of thinking.

- If you feel a need to criticize someone's behaviour, make sure that it is constructive criticism without allocating blame. For example, try saying: 'I feel irritated when you don't let me finish my sentence' instead of: 'You're really annoying – you're always interrupting me.' This second remark will only anger the other person, which does not resolve the problem.

- Be willing to look for alternative solutions to problems. Ask questions such as: 'Do you have any ideas how we can get around this problem?' Make sure that you listen carefully to any suggestions and do not dismiss them without due consideration.

Don'ts

There are two other types of verbal behaviour, either of which you may have used on occasions – passive or aggressive. These behavioural types are not helpful and, if used, will leave you feeling guilty or dissatisfied.

Look at the following examples of how *not* to tackle any situation. Have you used (or do you still use) any of these approaches?

PASSIVE VERBAL BEHAVIOUR

People who use this do the following.

- Frequently apologize as soon as they begin to speak. For example: 'I'm so sorry to be a nuisance but …'

- Speak in long-winded and rambling sentences which avoid getting to the point or making a request.

- Often use putdowns in their sentences, such as 'I'm an idiot', 'I'm hopeless' or 'I'm silly'.

- Constantly qualify any opinion they give with remarks such as 'It's only my idea – it's probably wrong' or 'I'm not really qualified to give my opinion but …'

- Give the impression that they have no choice when asking for something, such as: 'I'm afraid I have to ask you this'.

- Commonly dismiss their thoughts, requests or beliefs as unimportant. For example: 'It's of no interest but …' or 'It really doesn't matter but …'

- May stutter or fill uncomfortable silences with 'ums' and 'errs'.

- Rather than disagreeing, they will use words such as 'maybe' or 'sort of' to try and pacify someone who is not giving them the answer they are hoping for.

People who use this form of communication often have low self-esteem. They are putting the needs and feelings of others above their own and often do not give themselves any consideration at all. They have difficulty standing up for themselves and simply allow things to happen to them without opposition. Their overall objective is to please everyone and avoid any conflict.

Advantages to passive verbal behaviour

- You may receive gratitude from other people because you have satisfied their needs.

- You are less likely to be involved in any conflict.

- You may appear to be almost invisible and therefore not draw as much attention and resentment as aggressive personalities.

Disadvantages to passive verbal behaviour

- Your own needs are rarely met.

- You frequently have to do things which you feel unhappy about in order to placate others.

- You accept shoddy goods or poor treatment because you feel unable to complain.

- You build up feelings of resentment because it is too difficult to express your own needs.

- People begin to take advantage of your nature once they realize that you are not going to complain.

- You may be bullied or persecuted since you have assumed the role of a victim.

- Your levels of self-esteem and self-confidence will drop.

- You feel that you no longer have control over your life since other people dictate what you should do.

AGGRESSIVE VERBAL BEHAVIOUR

People who use this do the following.

- Often overemphasize their own importance and opinion. For example: 'I'm older than you and I can tell you that …' and 'Believe me when I tell you …'

- They tend to boast about how much better their life is. For example: 'Of course my health is excellent, whereas George has diabetes,' 'My old boss has serious debt problems whilst we are comfortably off' or 'My next-door neighbour's children have marital problems whereas ours are extremely happy.'

- They generally give clumsy, forceful advice, such as 'You know what you should do …' or 'Of course you've got to …'

- Give their opinions as facts, without stating that it is just their personal view. For example: 'Well we all know that was a really stupid thing to do' or 'Anyone will tell you that's an idiotic way to behave.'

- Are very judgemental and frequently point the finger of blame. For example: 'You really got that wrong didn't you?' or 'You're useless at this.'

- Use sarcastic comments to make their points. For example: 'Well aren't we the clever one?' or 'You must be stark raving mad if you think that's right.'

- Often use threatening questions to get their own way or make a point. These may include: 'What were you thinking when you did that?', 'Do you want to get into trouble?' or 'I need that now – where is it?'

- Also use threatening or intimidating comments to ensure that others complete tasks for them, such as: 'If you don't do that for me, I'll make your life miserable' or 'Complete this by tomorrow or else …'

Bullies (either at school, in the workplace or at home) often use aggressive verbal behaviour to intimidate others. Assertiveness can help you to deal with bullying behaviour in a calm and controlled manner.

People who use aggression to get what they want feel that winning is the most important factor. They will do anything to reach this goal, including hurting others. They will not show consideration for other people's needs or opinions and will use threats to get what they want. They may also use manipulation tactics to gain control of a situation. Emotional blackmail and even sulking are all different aggressive behavioural tactics.

Advantages to aggressive verbal behaviour

- There is only one possible advantage to this type of behaviour, which is that it may get you what you want in life.

Disadvantages to aggressive verbal behaviour

- Your lack of consideration for others will eventually cause them to stop communicating with you.

- People with good levels of self-esteem will, in turn, react in an aggressive manner as a response to your behaviour.

- Those who react passively will grow resentful and hostile over time.

- People who are prone to aggressive verbal behaviour often feel guilty afterwards, once they see how they have upset others with their behaviour.

- The effect that your aggression has on other people will ultimately affect your own level of happiness. Relationships will prove difficult to maintain since people will not want to spend time with you. Aggressive people are generally very unhappy since each new day brings the prospect of another series of battles which need to be won.

If you have developed a passive personality, try exploring your past. Have you always behaved in this way? It may be that this trait developed in response to someone else's behaviour. Living with an aggressive personality can lead some people to develop passive tendencies.

Exercise 13.2

Assertiveness

Now that we have examined each type of behaviour, take a moment to assess yourself. You may tend to use one type of behaviour in general or alternatively a mixture of all three (passive, aggressive and assertive).

During my anorexic years, I used passive behaviour almost without exception. Since recovery, I now always try to use assertive behaviour. This may not be possible in all situations though and I can still occasionally act in a passive or aggressive manner, which is perfectly normal. However, if you aim to use assertive behaviour as often as possible, you will soon begin to reap the benefits.

The following exercise outlines numerous difficult situations. Try to imagine how you would deal with each one in an assertive way, using the verbal behaviour which you have just read about. See if you can avoid a passive or aggressive reaction. You may feel that you would never encounter some of the suggested scenarios but try them anyway since it is all good practice for behaving assertively.

How would you react assertively in the following 16 situations?:

Public situations

- You receive the wrong meal in a restaurant. How do you send it back?

- You need to return an item of clothing to a store. The first time you wore the garment, it split. Can you explain the situation assertively to a young shop assistant?

- You are standing in a queue and someone pushes in front of you. What do you do?

- Your car is returned from the garage but it still has the same fault. How do you deal with this?

Home situations

You have a row with a member of your family because he has broken your mug. How do you resolve this?

- You overhear a family member criticizing you. How do you handle this?

- Everyone always expects you to do the housework. How can you make the workload more equal?

- It is Christmas and you are expected to visit relatives and join in with the festivities. You want to go out with your friends instead. Can you reach a compromise?

Work situations

- Your boss is giving you more work than you can handle. Do you stay late (doing unpaid overtime) or can you talk with him in an assertive manner?

- You make a serious error and someone else gets blamed for your mistake. Do you remain quiet or are you able to deal with the situation assertively?

- You are given the task of leading a team on a project. One of your workers is rude and disrespectful. How do you cope with this?

- You feel that a co-worker is flirting with you and you feel uncomfortable as a result. How do you get him to behave more appropriately?

Social situations

- You have lent £100 to a friend and now you are desperate for cash in order to pay the rent. Do you wait for her to remember or can you talk about this openly with her?

- You were ignored by a supposed friend on a night out and feel hurt. Do you pretend that it never happened or do you confront her directly?

- Your boyfriend keeps cancelling dates in order to meet his friend at the pub. Can you assertively tell him how you feel?

- A friend wants to borrow your car but you know that he is a bad driver. Do you allow him to borrow it and hope for the best or do you raise your concerns with him?

Advantages to assertive verbal behaviour

- You are more likely to satisfy your needs without upsetting either yourself or others.

- You are not abusing people (as with aggressive behaviour) or allowing them to take advantage of you (as with passive behaviour). The relationship here is equal.

- You feel that you have expressed your needs and opinions to the best of your ability rather than wishing you had said something different.

- Your self-esteem and self-confidence are boosted simply because you are able to verbalize your needs.

- Other people are more likely to respect you and speak assertively with you in return.

Disadvantages to assertive verbal behaviour

- Becoming assertive requires learning new ways of behaving and this is not always easy. The only way to master the technique is to keep practising so do not give up if you do not manage this approach the first time.

- Not everyone will want you to be assertive. There may be some people in your life who were happy for you to be passive. It was to their advantage that you constantly tried to please them and they will not want you to put your needs before theirs. However, such people are a negative influence and may be a part of the eating disorder.

- Some people may wrongly interpret assertiveness as aggression and might criticize you for being pushy. This is an incorrect analysis since when it is used correctly, assertiveness is all about ensuring that everyone's needs are met.

The needs form

The 'needs form' is a method of helping you to assertively work out how to meet each one of your needs. Whenever you feel that you have a specific need which has not been met, fill out this form and then follow your own instructions. The form is comprised of three sections.

- I need …

- What I would like to achieve …

- What steps should I take to achieve this?

A general example of this form might be as follows.

- I need … to gain some weight.

- What I would like to achieve … is to be able to eat without feeling afraid.

- What steps should I take to achieve this? Start practising exposure therapy and CBT. Ask for help if I am struggling.

A more specific example of this form would be as follows.

- I need … to phone the garage about the car.

- What I would like to achieve … is a car which has had its service.

- What steps should I take to achieve this? I can practise relaxation techniques beforehand to control my anxiety. I can also use CBT to remind myself that this is not a difficult or frightening task.

Chapter 14

Perfectionism

Perfectionism is a common trait amongst eating disorder sufferers. All of these illnesses are based on the idea of attaining the 'perfect' body. This will naturally lead to feelings of dissatisfaction and low self-esteem since it is impossible to achieve perfection.

This trait often begins in childhood, when a young person works hard to achieve high grades at school or to be the best at sports. In many cases, striving for perfectionism is viewed as a healthy, motivational attitude which helps people to achieve their goals through competitiveness. This is often referred to as 'positive' perfectionism.

However, the need to be perfect often turns obsessional and this leads to the development of negative behaviours. Psychological problems such as obsessive compulsive disorder, depression, panic disorders and eating disorders (such as bulimia and anorexia) can all feature perfectionism as a core symptom. This kind of unhealthy perfectionism is frequently referred to as 'clinical' or 'dysfunctional' perfectionism.

It is often a child's upbringing which affects his or her behaviour in later life. Parents who are distant or neglectful can lead their child to strive to be perfect. These children often feel that if they were the perfect child then their parents would love them. However, they are not able to alter their parents' attitude through this behaviour, which then often reinforces the idea that they are not good enough yet.

This pattern of behaviour is learnt early in life and may be replicated for years. Whenever they like someone, they will try to impress that person with their achievements. They are likely to become 'people-pleasers', matching their behaviour to the needs of those around them. If they feel that they have not pleased people enough then they brand themselves as a failure. Trying to win love in this manner generally leads to further emotional pain and rejection. It is common for people-pleasers to be used as 'doormats' by those around them. It takes a very scrupulous person not to use a people-pleaser to his or her advantage.

The impulse to please others, combined with a need to be perfect, can understandably result in the development of an eating disorder. Our society puts forward the concept of an extremely thin woman as the perfect image. Svelte celebrities, glamorous models and film stars are adored by millions. If people already feel a strong need to be loved, they can imagine that being the perfect size will bring them the love and adoration that they crave.

Identifying unhealthy perfectionism

If you agree with five or more of the statements in Table 14.1, it is highly probable that perfectionism is having a negative effect on your life. It is most likely to be focused on your weight, shape and the food you eat. However, it will also spill over into other areas of your life. It is common for sufferers to consistently set themselves unrealistic targets which they can not possibly achieve. This then causes them to feel a failure which leads them to be self-critical, and as a result, their self-esteem drops.

Table 14.1 Identifying unhealthy perfectionism

Thought	Agree	Disagree
I always think that I could have done better		
I am constantly preoccupied with doing things correctly		
Whatever I do, it is never good enough		
I must continually strive to improve everything that I do		
I do not feel that I am a success		
I judge myself purely based on my achievements		
I always criticize myself for not doing better		
I have set standards so high that my goals cannot be reached		
I always focus on my perceived failures and not the successes		
I feel no pride in my achievements		

Identifying your own perfectionist behaviour

Behaviour usually becomes ingrained almost without us noticing. The next exercise will help you to become more aware of the ways in which perfectionism affects your life.

Exercise 14.1

Writing an essay

Write a short essay in which you answer the following questions.

- How do you show perfectionist behaviour in your life? (For example, do you feel uncomfortable if you leave the house without making your bed?)

- Is all of your perfectionist behaviour negative? Can you list any positive aspects?

- Do you know why you have developed this behaviour? (These might include childhood experiences, a trauma or parental influences.)

- How does it feel to be a perfectionist? Has it affected your self-esteem?

If you are having difficulty knowing what to include in your essay, it may help you to write out a list of advantages and disadvantages to being a perfectionist. For example:

- *Advantage*: I can sometimes produce high-quality work.

- *Disadvantage*: I feel tense and anxious a lot of the time.

When writing this essay, it will be helpful to look back at when the behaviour developed. There are deep-rooted psychological problems behind perfectionism, such as fears which have never been confronted or needs that have not been met. You may have a fear of losing control or of disappointing others, as well as a need for constant approval. It might be advantageous to talk with relatives to discover exactly when the behaviour began. However, do be aware that it is possible

Perfectionism

that your family may have contributed to the development of this unhealthy behaviour.

I developed perfectionist traits, as well as a people-pleasing nature. Therapy helped me to identify the roots of this behaviour. I had been mentally abused by my grandmother from a very early age. Derogatory comments and consistently cruel behaviour had dramatically lowered my self-esteem. This was exacerbated by other family members who not only failed to protect me from this cruelty but actually encouraged me to continue visiting my grandmother even though they knew what was taking place.

As a young child, I tried to please others and this behaviour grew stronger as I grew older. By the time I was anorexic, I believed that I was responsible for everyone else's feelings and that it was my job to make them happy. This was very convenient for everyone around me and gradually I was blamed for anything that went wrong.

For example, my mother frequently told me that I was responsible for causing her migraines and on my twenty-first birthday, she said that I was ruining her and my father's lives. I took all of these comments on board and so tried even harder to please them and at the same time constantly punished myself for being such a bad person.

When I was 25, family therapy was set up since my therapists wanted to try and show my parents how I had learnt to take responsibility for everything negative. This did not work as intended though since my mother continually spoke of how difficult I was to live with. This resulted in my self-esteem dropping even further as the following diary extracts show.

Tuesday 6 August 1996

Mum spent a lot of time at therapy yesterday, talking about how I take up too much space in the food cupboard and how annoying this is for her. I saw my therapist Geoff today and told him how I was feeling.

I said all the things that Mum had been saying at therapy made me sure that she didn't love me. (At one session, she even said that she loved my brother Mark more than me.) I'm certain that's because I'm a horrible failure of a person and I never do anything right, no matter how hard I try to be the perfect daughter.

Geoff was very good. He said that even supposing I really did bad things and hurt people, I would never have meant to do this deliberately. This means that it still wouldn't have been my fault so I should not be blamed for it.

Thursday 18 April 1996

We had family therapy today and I've been left feeling that the anorexia is all my fault. Mum sat down at the session and before anyone else could speak, said: 'Anna has had this illness for so long now. When is it going to go? She's affected other people in the family but they've managed to get better so why can't she?'

I felt as though everything bad that has happened in the family is my fault. I tried to remember what my therapists had told me. They had said that the anorexia was caused by bad treatment and neglect when I was a child and that this was not my fault.

I wondered why Mum said these hurtful things at therapy. I knew the answer really though since a couple of days ago, she said to me: 'The therapists obviously only want to talk about you Anna and I thought "What about me?" "Why isn't anyone thinking about me?"'

Another common cause of perfectionism is a feeling of inferiority to a sibling. For much of my life, I felt a failure in comparison to my older brother Mark. My grandmother always favoured the male sons in my family and my mother constantly talked of my brother and his achievements. Years of always coming second led me to believe I was unimportant and my achievements were insignificant.

Saturday 15 June 1996

I felt hurt today by the way Mum treated me compared to the way she treats Mark. She is always so nice to him, gives him everything he asks for and puts him first. I've always thought that he was much more important that I was. Mum is so proud of him and with good reason – he is her successful child.

He has a good job, exhibiting gardens at the Chelsea Flower Show, a gorgeous six-month-old baby (her first grandchild) and a lovely wife. Mum tells everyone about them and is always showing photos of the baby. She is also always smiling whenever Mark asks for anything and she rushes off to get what he wants. If I ask for anything (and I try very hard not to) her face changes and she gets angry.

When Mark's around, I'm not even noticed unless Mum's feeling fed up and then I'm a convenient target to kick. It's understandable that she wishes I didn't exist – after all, I am the failure of the family. Maybe that's one of the reasons why I feel that I don't deserve food and want so desperately to disappear.

Sunday 7 July 1996

Mark and his family arrived today and I have to say that I've given up expecting Mum to be anything other than snappy with me. I don't know if it's deliberate but she's all over Mark and so nice to him and his family yet is really horrible to me.

I know she's worried about them coming and she wishes they weren't staying so long because she told me all this last night. But I wish she wouldn't give me such a hard time because it hurts. I feel such a failure as a person. I keep trying to be perfect, even when I'm feeling sad, but I'm just not good enough and that must be why people treat me the way they do.

Siblings can also be very competitive although it may be the case that only one side actually feels the competition. Although I am two and a half years younger than my brother, we both learnt to drive at the same time. My test date came through a couple of weeks before his, even though the applications were sent off at the same time.

One afternoon, a few days before my test was due, I was walking into the kitchen and overheard him say: 'I do hope that Anna doesn't pass her test because I don't want my younger sister to pass before me.' I quickly backed up so that no one saw me but I felt deeply upset. I should have confronted my brother at the time and said how I felt about his remarks but even at 17, I was too concerned with pleasing others all the time.

Siblings frequently have arguments and experience difficult times. They are naturally rivals for their parents' attention and will not necessarily enjoy each other's company. Teasing and even bullying is common between siblings, and if you feel that this is happening it is important to confide in someone who can help. However, it is a good rule not to allow sibling rivalry to affect your levels of confidence.

For many years, I based my self-esteem on my family's opinions of me and their behaviour towards me. As time passed, my self-esteem continued to drop since it was not beneficial to them to boost my confidence. Gradually, I grew to despise myself and wished that I was dead.

It is very dangerous to base all of your confidence and self-esteem on how other people treat you because it is possible that they may have an agenda. Self-confidence needs to come from within. Everyone occasionally hears a hurtful comment about themselves or is treated badly by a friend or relative. It is important to be able to ride these out without allowing them to destroy your self-esteem.

Family relationships can be difficult at times. People who we feel should be a positive force in our lives can sometimes have a negative influence. It is vital to recognize when this is happening so that you can protect yourself.

Learning to say 'No'

If you feel that you are a people-pleaser, one of the greatest lessons you can learn is how to say 'No'. I always felt that I could not say no to anything I was asked to do. I was certain that if I did then people would instantly hate me. I was very wrong about this point, however.

If people genuinely like you then they will respect the fact that you can say no from time to time. If people have been using you in any way because you never refuse their requests (asking you to do unpleasant jobs or letting you take responsibility for their mistakes) then they will not react as well. These are not the people you want in your life though since they are a negative influence.

Perfectionism activities

Once I had discovered why my need to be perfect had developed, I was able to start tackling the problem. I hope that the previous diary extracts illustrate how perfectionism can develop from childhood and early adult experiences. It does not have to be a permanent state though. The following activities show various different approaches that can help overcome these feelings.

- *Be realistic at work.* Perfectionism at work can be a hindrance since it reduces your flexibility, as well as affecting your ability to vary the speed and quality of your output. Bosses often require a task to be completed immediately and if you feel a need to continually re-do a task until you believe it to be perfect, it may take too long. Most jobs require efficiency and a good standard or work but not perfection since this is impossible in a busy workplace.

  Practise lowering your standards to a realistic level by deliberately working at 70 per cent of your normal level. This will feel extremely uncomfortable at first and you may need to use relaxation techniques to deal with the anxiety you feel. However, in time you will be able to accept that your work does not need to be 100 per cent perfect and you should find that this approach frees up extra time in which you can carry out the rest of your work with greater ease.

- *Set yourself time limits.* When you are trying to complete a task perfectly, it can prolong it indefinitely. You will always be able to find something which you believe needs changing or correcting. Try drawing a line under each task and say to yourself, 'That job is completed' even if you feel it could be improved. Before you begin a new task, set yourself a realistic time limit. Ask friends or co-workers how long a similar job would take them so that you can make an informed decision about how much time to allocate to this task.

  If it usually takes you an hour to clean the kitchen, divide this time in half. Allow yourself 30 minutes and then give each job a timescale: five minutes to do the washing up, five minutes for drying, five minutes to put away the dishes, five minutes to clean the cooker and so on. It is important to keep to these time limits, so you might want to set an alarm clock to help you at first.

- *Break your rules.* Perfectionist compulsions often cause sufferers to draw up complex rules and rituals. These are addictive habits which can quickly take over your life. Deliberately change something to break one of your rules and then use your preferred relaxation techniques to handle the resulting stress. The challenge is to cope with this anxiety (without altering the change you have made) until the level drops. If you can do this then the next time you make that change and break your rule, it will become slightly easier.

- *Share an imperfection.* Make a conscious choice to share one of your perceived weaknesses with a friend (such as the fact that you might have untidy cupboards). This exercise can help to show you that people will still like you, respect you and enjoy your company even if you are not perfect. You are also likely to discover that they are far more comfortable with the 'imperfect' you and frequently they will, in turn, share some of their own weaknesses as well.

- *Try to enjoy the world around you.* When you are constantly striving to be perfect, it can lead you to become self-absorbed. Take the time to enjoy the journey rather than always focusing on achieving a perfect end result.

Conclusion

Are you trying to force your life to be perfect? People place a lot of emphasis on trying to feel good all the time. Adverts attempt to convince us that the latest technology, clothes or cars will solve all of our problems. This creates unrealistically high expectations in people, who purchase these products in the belief that their lives will now be complete. People also look at others and feel that they are more fulfilled and having more fun. The author Edith Wharton once said, 'If only we'd stop trying to be happy, we could have a pretty good time.'

Often, feeling low is not necessarily a negative experience. It can help us to learn about ourselves and to understand our emotions more clearly. Do remember that we are all flawed human beings and cannot help but make mistakes from time to time. However, mistakes are a key part of life and they teach us lessons for the future. It is through our mistakes that we build vital knowledge and experience, as well as reminding us that total perfection is never possible.

If your aim is to be perfect, it is worth stopping to think what that would actually mean. No one could interact with a 'perfect person' (if this were actually possible) since that person would make everyone else feel inferior and insecure. How could anyone share their feelings and weaknesses with someone who could not relate to them? Would you really want to be this isolated and alone? Is it not better to be slightly flawed just like the rest of us?

Chapter 15

Building Confidence

Eating disorder sufferers often become withdrawn and isolated from the world. Food and weight are their sole focus and they grow secretive and suspicious of others. A key aspect of recovery is regaining lost self-confidence. This is a gradual process during which sufferers learn to like themselves again.

Behaviours such as laxative abuse, vomiting and bingeing result in them feeling self-disgust and self-hatred. Learning to accept that these behaviours are part of their illness can help sufferers to feel kinder towards themselves.

Recognizing one's good qualities is a helpful first step in rebuilding confidence. Sufferers may not believe that they even have any good qualities, and I know that this was true in my own case. I could list 20 things which I thought were wrong with me in a minute but I was unable to see anything positive.

Positive qualities

I learnt the following exercise during a stay in hospital. You can carry it out with a group of trusted friends, family or even your local support group.

Exercise 15.1

Positive qualities

Every person has a blank piece of paper stuck to his or her back. Once the exercise begins, everyone starts to walk around the room, stopping occasionally to write on each person's back.

They need to write about one of that person's positive qualities. When each person in the room has written one remark on the back of every other person, the exercise ends. Each person then has a sheet which lists his or her positive qualities as seen through other people's eyes.

At first, I found it very hard to believe all the positive things that people had written about me because my own opinion was so negative. The sheet of paper showed me that I was not as horrible as I had thought and I re-read these comments whenever I was feeling depressed.

You may also find it difficult to praise yourself and your own abilities. The next exercise allows you to practise this aspect of confidence-building. You will need to ask a close friend, relative or your therapist to help you with this exercise.

Exercise 15.2

Self-praise

Taking it in turns, each person has to say a sentence out loud which describes one of his or her good qualities. For example:

'I try to help other people when they are in need of support. That means that I am a kind person.'

This may be uncomfortable at first because praising ourselves can feel arrogant and self-satisfied. However, the purpose of this exercise is to show sufferers that they are not bad people. It is alright to ac-knowledge our good qualities in the same way as it is important that we recognize when we have made a mistake or behave in an unfair manner. Self-awareness allows us to view our whole personality instead of just the parts we choose to see.

Try to say out loud at least three good qualities which you recognize in yourself. Repeat this exercise (stating different positive qualities each time if possible) at least once a week until you feel more comfortable praising yourself.

It is not arrogant to accept your good qualities. There are many ways of speaking modestly about your talents, and talking about them will make you a more interesting and informative person. It is not easy to speak with people who constantly put themselves down at every opportunity.

Exercise 15.3

Choosing your qualities

It is not always easy to recognize what your best qualities are, so the following exercise addresses this problem. Listed below are a selection of different qualities ranging from positive to negative. You will need to pick out ten good qualities from these, which should be listed in order with your strongest quality at the top. You can then select two bad qualities which you believe that you have from the selection below. These should be the aspects of your life which you feel you need to work on.

Kind	Sulky	Helpful	Generous
Unkind	Receptive	Selfish	Manipulative
Careless	Miserly	Thoughtful	Thoughtless
Gentle	Friendly	Neat	Understanding
Aloof	Cheerful	Honest	Warm
Interested	Caring	Paranoid	Considerate
Passionate	Dedicated	Numb	Fickle
Enthusiastic	Critical	Imaginative	Narrow-minded
Spontaneous	Lively	Smug	Condescending
Patronizing	Friendly	Pushy	Gives compliments
Confident	Over-confident	Reassuring	Approachable
Dismissive	Comforting	Controlling	Indifferent
Calculating	Sensitive	Insensitive	Dismissive
Ethical	Possessive	Consistent	Two-faced
Self-serving	Forward-thinking	Determined	Loving
Brooding	Jealous	Intimidating	Cautious

Fearful	Intelligent	Artistic	Humourous
Bossy	Independent	Sympathetic	Treacherous
Imaginative	Brave	Aggressive	Passive
Trustworthy	Un-trustworthy	Self-obsessed	Entertaining
Fun	Supportive	Loyal	Disloyal
Empathic	Bigoted	Creative	Spiteful
Curious	Optimistic	Pessimistic	Competitive
Judgemental	Contented	Non-judgemental	Careful

There are other ways to build confidence as you are recovering, and many of them involve interacting with other people. Learning to mix in groups and with friends is good for self-esteem. When you can see that other people respond well to you, this can boost your confidence.

Eating disorder self-help groups can be beneficial for sufferers since they will be meeting people who experience similar problems. Overeaters can also choose to join exercise classes so that they gain support and encouragement with their weight loss.

Other groups that are unrelated to eating disorders, exercise or weight loss can also be a good way of meeting new friends and gaining confidence. Join an evening class which teaches a subject that you have never tried before, such as a new language or an artistic hobby. It may feel frightening to attempt this but often our fears only prevent us from moving ahead. These fears need to be acknowledged but they must not control your life. Push ahead with joining a club or class even if it feels wrong at first – it is important to take risks and try new activities.

Another problem which many eating disorder sufferers encounter during recovery is that they have forgotten how to enjoy themselves. They have stopped buying themselves treats because they do not feel that they deserve any pleasure. Try carrying out the following exercise once a week.

Exercise 15.4

Treat yourself

Buy yourself a non-food-related present. This can be anything you want from a magazine to a trip to the theatre. Make sure that you treat yourself to something different every week. Do not make this treat conditional – you should do this regardless of whether or not you have progressed in your recovery that week.

If you have a limited budget, select something cheap or even free. Pamper yourself with a long bubble bath. Choose a favourite book from the local library and allow yourself a whole evening off to enjoy it. Have some friends round. Hire a film. Just as long as it is something that you genuinely want to do.

Sufferers often feel depressed and this can make recovery more difficult. It is medically recognized that laughing can be highly beneficial to both physical and mental health. Hearty laughing causes the release of endorphins which help to lift the spirits.

There are groups in India which meet regularly to make themselves laugh. At first they have to force themselves (making the noises and pulling facial expressions without feeling the inner laughter) but after a short while, the absurdity of their situation soon creates natural laughter which is highly infectious.

Exercise 15.5

Laughter is the best medicine

If you feel unable to force yourself to laugh then allow comedy programmes to help you. Make sure that you watch at least half an hour of a favourite comedy show every day. Really allow yourself to enjoy the programme and laugh out loud. This can work just as well with radio shows or humorous books.

Before I met Simon, I watched very little comedy and did not really understand its appeal. However, it was a very important aspect of his life and I could soon understand why. Laughter can change your mood completely and for the better.

Chapter 16

Living at a Healthy Weight

Learning how to live at a healthy weight can be a very difficult stage of recovery for most eating disorder sufferers. Many feel frightened of reaching a safe weight for a number of different reasons.

- People may comment on how they look and compliment them on their weight gain, which might be misinterpreted.

- Once sufferers reach a healthy weight, other people often assume they are now recovered. They may not give them as much care and attention as a result.

- They will lose their 'eating disorder identity'. This is what currently makes them different to other people and why they may feel special.

- They will initially have to cope with feeling that they are 'fat' until they adjust to living at a normal healthy weight.

These are just four of the reasons why weight gain is so intimidating for sufferers. In exercise 16.1, try describing how you personally feel about reaching a healthy weight. Is it something you are looking forward to achieving or is it actually a frightening prospect? Give as many reasons as possible to explain why you are feeling this way.

What is my ideal weight?

Whether you are bulimic or anorexic, you are unlikely to be able to set your own healthy weight level. The majority of sufferers will always set their target weight too low. If you are serious about recovering then you need to accept that full recovery only comes about when you can maintain a healthy adult weight.

Sufferers often want to recover but at the same time also want to retain a low weight. This is not possible, however. When their body is underweight, sufferers' minds will cause them to focus on food constantly – this does not happen for people at a healthy size. From time to time during the day, they will naturally feel hungry and may think about food then. However, since their body is not starving, their preoccupation will be fleeting and as soon as they have eaten, their mind will move on.

All doctor's surgeries, health clinics and dieticians will have weight charts available. Using information that you provide about your age and height, your doctor (nurse or dietician) will be able to show you the ideal weight for your height. This target may feel quite a daunting prospect at first but remember that this is the weight at which you are most likely to avoid a relapse. This is also the

Exercise 16.1

My feelings about recovery

_____

_____

_____

_____

_____

_____

_____

_____

_____

_____

_____

weight at which you will be able to gain freedom from your disorder and can start to plan the rest of your life.

We all have a natural weight level and it is only when you are eating a full, healthy diet (without any restrictions) that you will discover exactly what this is. It will be within the weight range for your height but it could be a little higher or lower than your original target. It is important not to be intimidated by this prospect and to accept that this is true for most of us. In the same way that we can not change what colour of skin we are born with, we also cannot change our body type. It is this body type which dictates our natural weight level.

When you are recovering, it is easy to become obsessed with your target weight. Try to see this target not as numbers on a scale but rather as a measure of your physical health. The closer you get to your target weight, the healthier your body will become. Bones which had thinned due to malnutrition will begin to strengthen. Hair and nails will start to grow at a healthy rate and internal organs will rehydrate.

Although it is vital for anorexia sufferers to reach a healthy weight, it is also an important factor in recovery for both bulimia sufferers and compulsive overeaters. If you are suffering from bulimia, it is possible that your weight is currently at a normal level. However, you are likely to have experienced dramatic weight swings, ranging from underweight (during periods of starvation) to over-weight (when you are bingeing).

This yo-yo effect is extremely unhealthy and so it is equally vital that you aim to maintain your weight steadily at its natural healthy level. You are also far less likely to trigger the binge/vomit cycle if you are eating proper meals at regular times during the day. Binges commonly involve high-fat, high-sugar foods. The body craves these items when it has not received enough calories.

It is also healthy for compulsive overeaters to follow an eating plan which involves five or six smaller meals a day. When overweight people choose to diet, they often begin each day resolved to change their life from that point on. As a result, they may decide to avoid breakfast since this will lessen their caloric intake.

However, this is a mistake since a healthy high-fibre breakfast kickstarts the metabolism and fills the stomach, preventing later hunger pangs. Complex carbo-hydrates are a good energy source which are released slowly throughout the morning. If breakfast is ignored, by 11 am, anyone would be hungry and a craving for biscuits or a cake can trigger a binge.

Compulsive overeaters need to reach a healthy weight since this can improve their health and dramatically reduce the risk of further problems, such as diabetes or heart disease developing. However, it is not always easy for overweight people to live at a healthy weight since their size can sometimes act as a protection for them. For example, sexual abuse or rape can cause some women to try and make their bodies less attractive to men. This may seem like a solution at the time but sadly they are just punishing themselves further by endangering their health. If you feel that you have deliberately increased your size, it is important to seek help. If you try to decrease your weight to a more normal level, you may find that you experience the return of traumatic issues and need some support to help deal with these.

Assessing your true size

Most anorexia sufferers have an unrealistic view of their body size. When your weight drops below a particular level, your mind starts to grow distorted. Instead of looking in the mirror and seeing a thin person, the distortion leads them to see an overweight image of themselves. It can be helpful to learn exactly what size your body really is and the following two exercises should help anorexia sufferers.

Exercise 16.2

Clothing

Write down exactly what size you think you really are:

I think my size is…

If you have written 'extra large' or a woman's UK size 18 or 20 (USA sizes 16 and 18), you need to accept that these are large sizes.

Go into a department store and try on a jumper that is a size 18 (US size 16). Does it fit snugly? If it is even just a little baggy then this means that you are not this size. Then go down a size to 16 (US size 14) and repeat this exercise. Keep trying on clothes until you find a size which actually fits your body and does not hang loose at any point.

If you are anorexic, your distorted thinking will have led you to believe that you are large. If you have carried out the above exercise honestly then it is likely you fitted into a size 10, 8 (US size 8, 6) or even lower. These are all very small sizes – the average woman in the UK is currently size 16 (US size 14). A UK size 12 (US size 10) is considered slender and a UK size 14 (US size 12) would fit a woman of a healthy weight.

You have already gathered many facts to prove that you are not 'fat'. Overweight people can not fit into a UK size 10 or 8 (US size 8 or 6). This is another exercise which can help you to recognize that you are underweight.

Exercise 16.3

Comparisons

Do you have a friend (or therapist, nurse, dietician or similar) who is a healthy weight? Choose someone in your life who is comfortable with his or her body shape and size. It is important that this person is at a healthy weight for his or her height because you are going to compare measurements.

Using a tape measure, record a number of different measurements from various parts of the body (e.g. round the waist, top of the thigh, round the bust area). Make sure that you are together when you take both sets of measurements – one set from your friend and one from yourself.

Now compare the results. As an anorexia sufferer, your measurements are going to be much smaller. You now have another piece of evidence with which to fight your belief that you are overweight. How can you be 'fat' if your results are smaller than a person who is a normal, healthy size?

This diary extract shows how true evidence can help challenge entrenched anorexic beliefs.

Thursday 3 July 1998

I really don't understand what goes on in my head. I needed to buy some new jeans and I saw some in this catalogue a while ago, so I thought I'd order a pair just to see what they were like. The catalogue was very good and it had sizes from a really small 6 [US size 4] upwards. I ordered three different sizes because I really haven't got a clue what size I am.

They came today and I was really shocked because even the size 6 jeans were much too large for me. What totally confuses me is the fact that I feel so colossally fat all the time and even more gross and huge when I eat.

Why do I feel like that when I've got evidence that I'm not? Perhaps someone switched the labels at the catalogue warehouse and these are really a size 16 [US size 14].

You need to educate your logical mind into accepting the truth about your size. It is only the anorexia that wants you to believe that you are overweight and you need to challenge these dysfunctional beliefs which are holding you back.

Allow other people who genuinely care to reassure you if you are feeling badly about your body. *Listen* to their words and let them be a tool that you can use to fight the illness. *Do not* dismiss them as 'people who are just being kind' – this is the anorexia leading you astray again. People who care will tell you the truth about your size.

The benefits of living at a healthy weight

The major benefit for all eating disorder sufferers is that food will gradually no longer be an issue. When I began to recover, I did not believe that there would ever be a time when I did not count calories. Six months after I had reached a healthy weight, I suddenly realized that I no longer counted calories and had not been doing this for some time.

I was eating a normal healthy diet each day and eating food at regular intervals had meant that my body no longer constantly craved calories. As my body was satisfied, my mind did not need to dwell on food all the time. I felt physically stronger and was able to begin many new projects, both in terms of work and hobbies. There was not enough time in the day to fit in all the new interests which I now had.

One of my strongest reasons for holding on to the eating disorder was that without it, I might be just an empty person without an identity. Yet here I was just six months into recovery, with my life fuller and more satisfying than it had ever been.

As you recover and your physical health improves, your energy will return. Harness this vitality and put it into all of the projects and ideas which you previously shelved because of your disorder. Fill your mind with interesting hobbies and plans instead of focusing purely on food and weight issues. These are dead-end roads which can only lead you to unhappiness.

Am I recovered when I reach a healthy weight?

Attaining a healthy weight for your height is only the first step in recovery. Many hospitals discharge eating disorder patients when they reach their target weight, although this is frequently when they need the most support and encouragement.

Do not stop following your healthy eating plan when you achieve your target weight but continue to eat the set amount at set times for a number of months. You will know when you feel comfortable enough around food to pick up a snack bar without worrying how many calories it contains. Or when you want to try something new and different from your usual meals, regardless of its fat content or caloric value.

I remember looking at my partner Simon's pizza and then looking at my egg salad with disappointment. For the first time in years I chose to share a high-calorie meal because I found it more appealing. When I was in the early stages of recovery, I found it difficult to allow myself to eat a whole packet of savoury snacks or a bar of chocolate. However, if Simon was eating one of these, I found myself having small pieces of his snack. For about six months, Simon did not get to eat a full meal or snack since I was starting to try foods which I had considered unsafe for many years.

It can often feel far less intimidating to have a few nibbles from someone else's plate and it is a good way of reintroducing a new food back into your diet.

Can I begin exercising now that I am at a healthy weight?

Physical exercise is an important part of a healthy lifestyle, although it is important for recovering anorexia sufferers to take it gently and not exceed recommended levels. Exercise addictions can easily develop and, at this point in your recovery, it is not helpful to exchange one disorder for another.

The body utilizes 75 per cent of your daily caloric intake simply for staying alive, that is, keeping the heart pumping, the stomach digesting food, staying warm or cooling down and so on. This leaves only 25 per cent for all of your daily activities, which is why you must regulate your exercise.

Guidelines indicate that three 20–30-minute aerobic exercise sessions a week are highly beneficial. During this period, it is important to do some cardiovascular exercise so as to raise the heart rate. It is also advised that you do some muscle strengthening exercises twice a week.

Some recovering eating disorder sufferers find yoga useful since this is a form of exercise which also incorporates relaxation techniques. It can be taken at a gentle pace and also allows a person to become more aware of his or her body as well as becoming more attuned to it.

Avoid extreme forms of exercise, such as marathons, skiing, skateboarding or mountaineering, because these will place too much strain on a body which has recently been physically traumatized by starvation or bingeing and purging, or both.

Why do I have trouble accepting compliments?

When you reach a healthy weight, you are likely to find that people start to compliment you on how well you are now looking. This often feels like a very negative experience for anorexia sufferers since they equate the term 'healthy' with 'fat'. This is not the intended message that is being put forward by other people – they are genuinely relieved to see that you are looking well.

Anorexia sufferers cannot see how ill they appear when they become emaciated but their family and friends can. Owing to the secretive nature of the disorder, people close to a sufferer often feel unable to express their fears and distress at the sufferer's appearance. It is only when recovery takes place that they feel comfortable enough to make any comments.

Use CBT to help you deal with compliments such as: 'It is lovely to see you looking so well.' If you interpret this in a negative way to mean: 'You look so fat today' then challenge this with positive logic. Remind yourself that it is only anorexic thinking which is trying to convince you that you are overweight. This person is genuinely complimenting you on looking healthy.

When you reach a healthy weight, it can be helpful to look at your life and change

Exercise 16.4

Role-play

It can often be helpful to practise potentially difficult situations in advance. Ask a friend, relative or even your therapist to practise giving you compliments so that you can learn how to accept them gracefully without slipping into depression.

When you have low self-esteem, it is often tempting to dismiss a compliment rather than accepting it. This can be very hurtful to the other person, however. For example:

Person A: 'You look really lovely tonight. What a gorgeous dress.'

Person B: 'You must be joking. I look like a pink hippo. I'm so revolting.'

It may be tempting to vocalize your insecurities and feelings of distress but sometimes it is not the right situation. Your comments are likely to offend or upset the other person since you are effectively dismissing his or her opinion and throwing the compliment back at that person.

If it is difficult during role-play to accept a whole series of compliments then alternate roles with your practice partner until it begins to feel more comfortable.

any part of it which leads to eating disorder behaviours. For example, reading fashion magazines can be difficult since the pages are filled with photos of underweight models.

You may also feel that this would be a good time to join a self-help group. Remember that reaching a healthy weight is only the beginning of your recovery and it can help to share your thoughts and feelings with other sufferers. Hearing that their experiences are similar to your own and learning how they cope and have moved on with their lives can be extremely useful.

Try to build up a support network so that you have people who you can call on for help if you are feeling low. Do not end all of your therapy as soon as you reach a healthy weight – it can be very beneficial to continue learning about yourself and the reasons you behave the way that you do.

Discovering more about your childhood and how your relatives behaved can also be extremely enlightening. For example, you might discover that your mother had a poor body image and often commented negatively about herself. Early influences such as this can have a strong effect on adult behaviour.

Learning to like yourself inside and out

Eating disorder sufferers often say that they hate themselves. They dislike both their body shapes and their personalities in general. A large part of recovery is learning how to be kinder to yourself. You have treated yourself badly for a long period and now it is time to reverse this damaging attitude.

Many of these body image problems stem from constant comparisons. Television programmes, ·films and magazines are full of images of stick-thin celebrities. Instead of looking at these people as role models, try to see them as a highly unusual group within society.

Look outside your door at the people on the street. Do any of them resemble film stars? Extensive surgery, personal trainers, dangerous diets and even medications have been used by stars to force their bodies into unnatural shapes. Magazines and newspapers contain many tell-all stories from stars who have since realized the damage they have done to themselves as a result.

The healthy choice is learning to like the body you have instead. For example, start to choose clothes that flatter your shape rather than hide it.

The following is an exercise to help you accept yourself and learn to respect your own qualities and assets.

Exercise 16.5

Acceptance

Write a list of all your good qualities. Be sure to include every talent and achievement. Try not to leave anything out – this list can be as long as you want to make it. Include a section showing recent compliments which people have paid you.

My good qualities

_____

_____

_____

_____

_____

_____

_____

_____

When you have completed your list, keep it to hand. You may even want to stick it on a wall. Turn to this list whenever you are feeling bad about yourself. If you do something wrong and begin shouting negative remarks at yourself (such as 'You're so useless – you never do anything right') turn to your list for reassurance.

Go to your chart and read through the list of all the good things you do regularly. This will help show you that the feeling of negativity is wrong. You might have done something wrong today but that does not mean that you are a 'useless' person. It just means that you made a mistake – something we all do on a daily basis.

Chapter 17

Coping with Setbacks

All eating disorder sufferers will experience some setbacks during their recovery, which are likely to make them feel distressed. This may be due to their having a perfectionist nature (something very common among sufferers). Setbacks are quite normal though and they can teach us how to tackle difficult issues during recovery.

However, setbacks are not the same as relapses (where sufferers choose to give up their recovery entirely and return to their eating disorder). When you are taking baby steps forwards towards recovering, you will almost inevitably take some baby steps backwards during certain stages in the process. It is important not to be discouraged if this happens.

You can try to avoid setbacks by planning ahead. If you are aware that a difficult situation is likely to cause you to take steps backwards, try to plan a coping strategy. During the early stages of my recovery, I found that there were numerous events or scenarios which could lead me to restrict my diet or overexercise again. These included:

- reading women's magazines

- trying on clothes in department stores

- eating a meal with a friend who was on a diet

- family celebrations which involved food, such as a barbecue or birthday party

- conflict with others

- changes in my weight.

Over time, I gradually developed a coping strategy for each of these situations so that I managed to avoid taking steps backwards.

For example, I knew that trying on jeans in department stores often led to my feeling 'fat'. This was because every store or clothes label had slightly different measurements for their jeans. I could be one size in M&S and a completely different size in Top Shop.

I decided that I would order clothes from one particular catalogue until I felt more comfortable with my body. That way, I knew that the clothes would be a uniform size and I could try them on in my own home, which I found far less stressful.

Of course, some situations will arise which you have not planned for. These may place your recovery under additional stress and it is often helpful to ask for some extra help at times like these.

For example, when I was 18 months into my recovery, I fell ill with gastroenteritis. For six weeks, I was very sick and found it hard to eat. When I began to recover from this illness, I noticed that I had lost quite a lot of weight and my clothes were loose.

Exercise 17.1

Coping strategies

Try listing below some situations that you find stressful and which might test your recovery:

_____

_____

_____

_____

_____

_____

_____

Now make some plans to cope with those difficult events without resorting to negative eating-disordered behaviour patterns:

_____

_____

_____

_____

_____

_____

_____

I immediately felt elated since the eating disorder 'voice' praised me for my achievement. However, this was not a road I wanted to go down again. I realized the weight loss was caused by a serious illness and that I would gain back those lost pounds as soon as I started eating normally again.

Affirmations

When you are struggling with setbacks, it can help to remind yourself why you are fighting for recovery. I had a list of affirmations that were positive reminders of exactly what I was trying to achieve. The following are some examples that I used:

- My life will be my own without the eating disorder.

- I do not need to be thin for people to like me.

- Food will no longer control my life.

- My eating disorder is not my friend.

- Recovery is not always easy but it is so worthwhile.

- My eating disorder is stopping me from achieving my goals.

Try writing some of your own, which are especially relevant to your own life and goals.

Exercise 17.2

My affirmations

_____

_____

_____

_____

_____

_____

_____

_____

_____

_____

Analyse your setback

If you do have a setback, use it to your advantage and learn from it. It is important to get back on track as soon as is possible.

If for example you have skipped lunch and gone to the gym instead, do not wait until your next scheduled meal before eating again. If you normally have lunch at noon, try having it at 2 pm instead. Do not use a late lunch as an excuse to miss your mid-afternoon snack – you need to have that as well.

See if you can analyse the setback to find out why you behaved in this way. Try and remember your thought process before the setback:

- What were you thinking?

- Were they negative thoughts about yourself and your body?

- Had someone made a comment about your size? (Even a positive compliment from a friend can result in a setback.)

- Did something go wrong at work, school or home?

- Was someone angry with you for any reason?

You are likely to have felt out of control just before the setback. Using eating-disordered behaviours probably seemed like a way of regaining control or stability in your life.

It is important to write down as much information as possible. Below is an example from my own therapy.

- *Setback*: Didn't eat any dinner today and exercised for two hours.

- *Thoughts before setback*: I am getting too fat too quickly. I need to eat less and exercise more.

- *Incident that led to setback*: I had put on some weight this week and my therapist was pleased. She complimented me and said that I was looking much better.

- *What I should have done*: Talked through the negative feelings with my therapist. Recovery is not a smooth road. Weight goes on in different stages. It is *good* that I am looking better. I don't want to be ill all my life.

After I had worked through my negative thoughts, I made sure that I had a good meal to make up for the missed dinner and the intense exercise.

Conclusion

You are likely to have setbacks at all the different stages of recovery. If one occurs in the later stages, do not be afraid to return to the strategies that helped you to reach the stage you are at. You might find it useful to enlist help from a friend or return to a more rigid and structured eating plan for a while.

Many sufferers believe that they never completely beat their eating disorder. It is often there at the back of their mind and can return during times of great stress. I do not personally hold with this view.

Many years into my recovery, I have experienced numerous stressful situations and have never chosen to return to my eating disorder. It just seemed like an added complication which I did not need. I therefore believe that full recovery is quite possible (as I know from my own recovery and from the many ex-sufferers who contact me) and that setbacks need not plague you for life.

Be prepared for setbacks but do not let them spoil your recovery process. Use them to help you gain greater knowledge about your own recovery and remind yourself of the good progress that you have been making so far.

You will need to accept that recovery takes time though. It took many months or even years for your disorder to develop so it will not vanish overnight. It is also important to accept that you are likely to feel worse before you feel better. This was certainly true for me.

Do not feel upset if you have setbacks late on in your recovery. Try reading back through your earlier diary extracts to remind yourself how well you have done and how much progress you have made.

Also, as you begin to recover, you are likely to re-experience some of the feelings which led you to develop your eating disorder in the first place. While you have been ill, these emotions will have been buried by constant thoughts about food and weight.

As you progress in your recovery, you will encounter many new potential problems, such as relationships, work, where to live and so on. These problems are all a normal part of life but they are likely to seem quite intimidating at first.

I once explained my fears to a therapist and she smiled broadly, replying: 'Enjoy every one of your problems because they show how far you have come in your recovery and that you are an adult young woman.'

Chapter 18

Recipes for a Positive Approach to Food

Eating disorder sufferers often feel unable to allow themselves to eat certain foods. This section will show that no food type should be off-limits since they can all form part of a healthy diet. It also aims to give sufferers permission to begin to eat these foods again as part of their recovery. I naturally felt afraid whenever I had to eat new foods during recovery but it was still a relief to feel that I was allowed to have them.

It can help many sufferers to think of food as a medicinal part of their recovery. For example, some sufferers may have taken pills to help lighten their mood and food can be seen as a similar prescriptive treatment. All of the recipes in this section can be seen as medicine, which sufferers need to take in order to help them recover.

If you have been severely restricting your diet, it can feel extremely frightening to resume eating normally again. Begin slowly by eating food that is soft and easily digestible, such as:

- scrambled egg and mashed potato

- milk-based puddings like semolina, rice puddings, yoghurts, blancmange and custards

- breakfast cereals, such as porridge made with milk (cow's milk or soya milk is fine).

- pasta, noodles and rice are all good sources of carbohydrates and are easy to eat when combined with a tasty sauce. Start by eating the lower-calorie varieties of sauce, such as tomato, and gradually progress to the richer, creamier varieties.

Initially avoid choosing food that is harder to eat, such as crunchy toasted sandwiches or thick burgers. Intimidating food can cause sufferers to take steps backwards during the crucial early stages of recovery. Instead, select basic foods that you can adapt and increase as your recovery progresses. For example:

- Open sandwiches – these are very versatile since you can begin with a light chicken salad and then build up to alternative fillings like cheese and pickle or egg mayonnaise.

- Jacket potatoes – this is another healthy snack food which can be stuffed with a variety of fillings depending on how your recovery is progressing. You can choose from any of the following: cottage cheese, baked beans, tuna and mayonnaise, chilli or egg mayonnaise.

- Omelettes – these can be altered with ease to accommodate new ingredients. Start with a plain one and gradually add cheese, potato, vegetables, cold meats, Quorn or anything else you might fancy. Let your imagination run wild. As you recover, you will find that a Spanish omelette or tortilla makes a delicious meal.

It is likely that, as an eating disorder sufferer, you have focused on eating only low-calorie items. This is your choice, although remember that you are basing your progress on the number of calories consumed each day. If you are on a 1500-calorie per day diet, you will have to eat a large quantity of food if you choose only these low-calorie options. By selecting cheddar cheese instead of cottage cheese on a jacket potato, you will halve the volume of cheese you need to eat. If you are anorexic, this can be helpful at the start of recovery since your stomach will have shrunk from constant dieting.

Many people believe that eating disorder sufferers should not eat any diet products or low-calorie foods when they are recovering. I disagree with this view since diet foods can often bridge the gap between eating very little and resuming a normal diet. Sufferers will often have a limited diet when they first begin recovery and all new foods seem extremely intimidating. If they are willing to try a diet yoghurt then that is a good first step. They can then progress to higher-calorie desserts as they continue their recovery.

Another way to increase calories without adding another intimidating meal is the idea of 'snack pots'. Fill bowls with nuts, potato crisps, pretzels, cheese biscuits and so on, and then distribute them around the house. If there are small pots of nibbles to hand, sufferers can graze on a few at a time throughout the day. This allows them to eat extra calories in a gentler way.

It can also help sufferers to have five or six small meals a day rather than three large ones. Not only can large meals seem daunting but they also leave the sufferer feeling overfull and nauseous. Do make sure when dividing the daily calorie intake into smaller meals that they contain the equivalent number of calories to the original three meals.

Observe how healthy people eat. I used to watch people selecting food in a restaurant. They chose what they felt like eating rather than the lowest-calorie items on the menu. This showed me how free and easy people could be around food and this proved to me that this was possible to achieve.

Be honest. If you have had a day where you avoided food or chose only low-calorie options, admit this to yourself. Accept that you need to eat some extra calories. If you are finding eating too hard, choose a milkshake, Complan® or Build-Up-style drink to give your body the extra fuel that it needs. Going to bed hungry will lead to a disruptive night with the likelihood of night sweats and nightmares.

Dietary needs vary depending on the individual eating disorder. Bulimia sufferers, for example, may be low in potassium and other vital salts because of their constant bingeing and vomiting. Bananas are a good source of potassium to help counter this deficiency.

Consider asking your local doctor for vitamin and mineral supplements while your diet is still restricted.

Vegetarianism

It may be that you were a vegetarian prior to your eating disorder developing (as I was). However, many sufferers choose to become vegetarians as a way of cutting out extra food. If this is the case then you may want to consider whether you actually like eating meat or not. If the honest answer is 'yes' then part of your recovery should involve reintroducing this protein back into your diet. If you want to remain a vegetarian for ethical reasons or just because you genuinely dislike the taste of meat then this is fine. A good vegetarian diet is very healthy if followed correctly.

It is important to ensure that you are eating enough protein on this diet. Protein is found in the following types of food.

- *First-degree (or 'complete') protein units*: eggs, cheese and milk. (Not suitable for a vegan diet.)

- *Second-degree protein units*: beans, lentils, seeds, nuts, soya, peas, rice, pasta, potato and bread.

Potatoes and bread are also turned into complete protein units when eaten with nuts, lentils, seeds or beans. The following are examples of these combined protein unit meals:

- peanut butter sandwiches

- rice and beans

- vegetarian chilli with rice or bread.

Soya is another excellent source of protein and is extremely versatile. It is also available in other forms, such as:

- *Soya milk* – this contains between 4g and 10g of protein per cup.

- *Soya flour* – this can be used as an alternative to wheat flour in recipes for muffins, biscuits and brownies. Half a cup of flour contains 22g of protein.

Recipes and diet plans

The following recipe section includes a number of different suggestions to help get you started with your recovery. As you make progress, try to search out new foods and experiment with different meal ideas. Remember that this is just the beginning – it is up to you to design your diet plan according to your personal tastes (instead of the decisions made by the disorder). These diet plans and recipes are designed for adult women – male sufferers would need to add between 300 and 400 extra calories per plan.

As you start to recover, you will gradually be able to admit which foods you genuinely enjoy. I like cheese, but for many years I pretended that I did not to avoid having to eat it. Recovery is about trying all the foods that you enjoy.

When I was in hospital, the eating disorder sufferers were allowed to nominate two foods that we did not like. These two choices were then removed from our diets and we had to eat everything else that was provided. We were not allowed to exclude high-fat foods, such as chocolate and crisps, since many of the sufferers would have listed these foods in an attempt to avoid them. This was a good approach since it actually forced the sufferers to be honest.

Exercise 18.1

Disliked foods

Nominate two foods which you genuinely dislike. Think this through carefully because by nominating these two items, you are also agreeing to try all the other types of food available. This may seem a daunting prospect but remember that you are not going to be expected to eat them all in one day.

Various foods will gradually be introduced by yourself at your own discretion as your recovery continues. You might not yet be ready to design a healthy diet plan that will lead to your recovery. If this is the case, ask for help.

Your doctor may be able to refer you to a nutritionist who will be able to create an eating plan which is individually tailored to your needs. Alternatively, you may have a friend or relative who could advise you. If none of these ideas seems possible, try following one of the set calorie plans below. Choose the one that is most suited to your caloric and dietary needs.

Sample diet plans
1200 calories per day

- *Breakfast*: 30g cereal; 1 glass of skimmed milk; 1 banana or 1 yoghurt.

- *Lunch*: Chicken salad (made with 4oz of chicken); this can be alternated with Quorn, ham, cheese or egg; 1 soft roll (buttered).

- *Snack*: 1 apple or yoghurt.

- *Dinner*: low-fat omelette (see recipe section); salad and a baked potato; fruit for dessert (e.g. strawberries).

- *Late night snack*: milky drink (such as hot chocolate); digestive biscuit.

1400 calories per day

- *Breakfast*: toasted English muffin with tablespoon of cream cheese (2 tablespoons if low-fat); 1 glass orange juice; 1 yoghurt.

- *Lunch*: turkey and salad sandwich (using 2 slices of wholemeal bread and low-fat spread); 1 banana.

- *Snack*: 1 pear.

- *Dinner*: 1 portion of mushroom bolognese; salad; yoghurt.

- *Late night snack*: milky drink (such as hot chocolate); digestive biscuit.

1600 calories per day

- *Breakfast*: 1 serving of raisin and cinnamon porridge (see recipe); 1 glass orange juice.

- *Lunch*: vegetable burger (or chicken burger) in a sesame seed bun (including 1 tablespoon of mayonnaise); salad with optional dressing; fresh fruit salad.

- *Snack*: 1 fruit cereal bar.

- *Dinner*: stuffed mushrooms (see recipes); jacket potato; salad; yoghurt.

- *Late night snack*: milky drink (such as hot chocolate); digestive biscuit.

1800 calories per day

- *Breakfast*: 2 slices of toast with 2 teaspoons of margarine; 1 boiled, poached or fried egg; yoghurt and a bowl of strawberries.

- *Snack*: muesli bar.

- *Lunch*: jacket potato with 2oz cheddar cheese; salad; banana.

- *Snack*: peach; 2 plain biscuits.

- *Dinner*: portion of vegetable rice (see recipes); 3 oz chicken or fish or 2 Quorn fillets; fresh fruit salad.

- *Late night snack*: milky drink (such as hot chocolate); digestive biscuit.

These are only sample plans, however. It is up to you to design one that is best suited to your own needs. It is likely that you are highly knowledgeable about calories, so use this to help with your recovery. Design a workable plan that will help you gain weight to a healthy level (or lose it if you are a compulsive overeater).

Naturally, there are an endless number of ways that you could cheat on your plan, although remember that this recovery is for you and the only person you would hurt by cheating is yourself.

Please also note that these diet plans are only estimates – it is impossible to be precise since many products contain differing calorie contents. No two pots of yoghurt are identical throughout the various brands, for example. However, do try to avoid choosing the smallest apple or the lowest-calorie cereal since this is just allowing the eating disorder to control your choices.

Gradually, as you move on in your recovery, try to phase out the constant calorie counting. If you feel like a chocolate bar then have one but do not try to compensate for it by cutting down on calories later in the day.

These sample diet plans can help any eating disorder sufferer. If you are anorexic, start with the lowest-calorie plan and gradually keep moving on to the next plan at a pace that you feel comfortable with.

If you are suffering with bulimia then your diet plan needs to help you maintain your blood sugar level. If this drops and you feel hungry, you may start bingeing and this will then trigger vomiting and purging. A healthy adult woman requires approximately 1950 calories per day to maintain her weight. Make sure your plan contains the correct number of calories to help you recover.

If you are suffering from compulsive overeating then it is possible that you are overweight and are trying to diet. Use these plans in reverse order, starting with the 1800 calorie plan and then gradually cutting down on your food intake. If you attempt a low-calorie diet immediately, it is likely that you will feel very hungry and this could trigger binges. Remember that slow weight loss is far more likely to be permanent than sudden drops.

Possible recipes
Cheese and potato fritters (serves four)

Ingredients

500g (1¼ lb) potato	Salt and pepper
115g (4oz) cheese	1 beaten egg
4 spring onions (chopped)	3 tablespoons olive oil
1 tablespoon lemon juice	Flour for dredging

Boil the potatoes in their skins until soft. Drain the water and peel the potatoes. Place in a bowl and mash. Grate the cheese into the potato and add the spring onions, lemon juice and egg. Season to taste.

Place the bowl containing the mixture into the fridge until it is chilled and firm. Divide the mixture into walnut-sized balls then flatten them slightly and cover with the flour. Heat the oil in a frying pan and fry the fritters. Cook until they are brown on each side. Drain on kitchen paper and serve at once with salad or vegetables.

Since this recipe serves four people, make sure that you have one-quarter of the finished fritters.

Vegetarian mini pizzas (serves one)

Fast food often appears on many sufferers' 'bad food' lists as it is considered to be high in fat, sugar and salt. However, no food should be classified as 'bad' because then there is the risk that it will either become a binge food or be eliminated from your diet altogether. Sufferers may feel unable to incorporate fast foods into their diet at the beginning of their recovery. It is therefore helpful to make healthier versions of these foods so that they are no longer considered forbidden.

Ingredients

4 large mushrooms	2 English muffins (split in half)
1 orange, red or yellow pepper	or crusty rolls if preferred
1 tablespoon olive oil	125ml (4fl oz) tomato sauce
1 tablespoon mixed herbs	125g (4oz) Mozzarella cheese
	(or any cheese you prefer)

Heat your grill to the highest setting. Remove the grill pan and line with foil. Clean the mushrooms and then slice thinly. Core, seed and slice the pepper.

Place the mushroom and pepper slices in the grill pan. Drizzle them with the olive oil and then sprinkle on the dried herbs. Using your hands, gently mix everything together in the pan so that the vegetables are evenly coated with oil and herbs.

Spread out the vegetables in the pan and place the muffins (uncut side up) on the side of the pan. Grill for five minutes until the muffins are toasted and the vegetables have softened.

Remove the muffins from the pan and continue to grill the vegetables until they are soft and tender. This should take another two minutes. Spread the muffin halves with tomato sauce and then add the vegetable mix.

Chop the Mozzarella cheese and divide evenly between the pizzas. Place the mini pizzas back under the grill for approximately three to five minutes until the cheese has melted.

This meal can be served with a salad and provides three essential food groups – carbohydrates, vegetables and protein. Try to avoid selecting a very low fat cheese since this will not necessarily cook as well on the muffins.

Stuffed mushrooms (serves one)

Sufferers often feel that it is alright to eat fruit and vegetables. It is naturally healthy to eat a certain amount of fruit and vegetables every day, although this needs to be in conjunction with other types of food. The following dish includes cheese to provide protein but mostly consists of vegetables, so is not too intimidating for sufferers.

Ingredients

4 large Portobello mushrooms
1 garlic clove (optional)
1 red, green or yellow pepper
Half an onion

Olive oil
Salt and pepper
50g (2oz) grated cheese

Heat the oven to 180°C / 350°F / Gas Mark 4. Peel and finely chop the garlic clove. Core, seed and cut the pepper into 0.5cm (quarter-inch) pieces. Peel and finely chop the onion so that the pieces are of a similar size to the pepper. Separate the mushroom stalks from the tops. Finely chop the stalks.

Heat two tablespoons of olive oil in a large frying pan over a medium heat. Add all the chopped vegetables into the pan and stir frequently. Keep on the heat for three to five minutes until the onions and peppers are soft. Remove the mixture from the pan and set to one side.

Heat another two tablespoons of oil in the pan. Add the mushrooms to the pan (gill side down) and fry for five minutes until the mushrooms begin to soften. Remove from the heat and place the mushrooms on a baking tray, gill side up.

Equally divide the vegetable mixture between the four mushrooms. Bake in the oven for approximately ten minutes or until the vegetable filling is hot and the mushroom flesh is tender when poked with a knife. Sprinkle the cheese evenly over the mushrooms and serve.

Raisin and cinnamon porridge (serves one)

Porridge is another food that is easy to eat and digest. It is quick to make and, if served with milk, this version provides protein, carbohydrates and fruit.

Ingredients

150ml (5fl oz) milk
100g (4oz) porridge oats
25g (1oz) raisins or sultanas

A pinch of salt
Cinnamon to taste
Brown sugar to taste

Put the milk, porridge, raisins and salt in a pan over a high heat and bring to the boil, slowly stirring all the time. Lower the heat and allow the porridge to simmer for four to five minutes until thick and creamy.

Stir in the cinnamon to taste. Serve in a bowl and sprinkle with brown sugar.

Low-fat omelette (serves one)

This is a low-fat and low-calorie meal. At only 160 calories, one serving can make a good meal for sufferers (especially anorexics) who are just starting their recovery programme.

Ingredients

4 egg whites
1 tomato (chopped)
4 tablespoons milk
50g (2oz) grated cheddar cheese

$\frac{1}{2}$ cup sliced mushrooms
$\frac{1}{2}$ cup sliced onions
Low-fat vegetable spray for frying
Salt and pepper for seasoning

Beat the egg whites together with the milk and season to taste. Set this to one side. In a separate dish, place the mushrooms, onions and two tablespoons of water.

Cover the dish and microwave it for two to three minutes (depending on whether you like soft or crunchy vegetables). If you prefer, the mushrooms and onions can be cooked in a pan with a little oil until brown and slightly crispy.

If you microwaved your vegetables, drain off the water. Add the chopped tomato and cooked vegetables to the egg mixture. Heat a frying pan with a small amount of oil or several sprays from a low-fat vegetable spray.

Add the egg and vegetable mixture and cook on a medium heat. When the eggs begin to set, sprinkle on the cheese and allow it to melt. When the omelette appears cooked but moist, fold it over on one side and gently lift onto a plate.

If you find that your omelette sticks to the pan, this means that you have not used enough oil. If you are struggling to cope when oiling a pan because of the extra calories involved then ask someone else to do this for you (I know that I had difficulty with this at first).

Your omelette should be served with something else, depending on where you currently are in your recovery:

- *early days*: salad

- *mid-point*: boiled potatoes and salad

- *nearing full recovery*: chips and salad.

Scrambled eggs (serves one)

When a sufferer starts to eat again, it can feel very daunting. Foods that are easy to eat and to digest are preferable. The following recipe is both nutritional and tasty without being too much hard work.

Ingredients

2 eggs

12g ($\frac{1}{2}$oz) butter or margarine (or 1 tablespoon of sunflower or olive oil)

Salt and pepper to taste

Optional: 50g (2oz) button mushrooms, Quorn pieces, bacon bites, smoked salmon or any vegetable of choice

Break the eggs into a bowl and beat until well blended. The longer you beat the eggs, the lighter the finished product will be. Season with salt and pepper to taste.

Melt the butter or oil in a frying pan on a medium heat and swirl it around so that the whole pan is covered. When the butter or oil is lightly sizzling, add the beaten egg.

Use a spoon or fork to stir the eggs continually until they are thick and creamy. Just before they look fully cooked, remove the pan from the heat and serve on a plate. The eggs will continue to cook for a further 30 seconds in their own heat. If they are left on the heat until fully cooked, this would result in dry scrambled eggs.

To make a variety of different scrambled egg dishes, follow the instructions below.

- *With button mushrooms*: trim and brush the mushrooms until clean. Heat the butter or oil in the pan and fry the mushrooms until lightly golden. If necessary, add a little more oil and then add the egg mixture. Cook as before.

- *With quorn, bacon bites, smoked salmon or vegetables of choice*: add to the egg mixture and cook as before.

Mashed potatoes (serves two)

Ingredients
2 large potatoes
Salt
Knob of butter or margarine

Peel the potatoes, chop and place in a pan half-full of water. Bring to the boil and then turn down the heat so that the water gently bubbles. The potato will take anything from ten minutes to half an hour to cook, depending on the variety of potato used. Test it frequently with a knife to feel if the potato is soft.

Once cooked, drain away the water. Add the salt and butter (or margarine) and mash with a fork or masher until the potato is fluffy.

Cheese and tomato potato wedges (serves four)

Ingredients
4 large cooked potatoes
Olive oil
Sea salt

350g (12oz) jar of tomato sauce for pasta
125 g ($4\frac{1}{2}$oz) grated cheddar cheese

Pre-heat the oven to 200C / 400F / Gas Mark 6. Cut four large cooked potatoes into wedges. Place the wedges into a roasting tin (skin side down). Drizzle over a little olive oil and a sprinkling of sea salt. Bake in the oven for 10 minutes.

Remove from the oven and spoon a full 350 g jar of pasta sauce over the wedges. Then sprinkle the grated cheese and return the dish to the oven. Cook for a further 10 minutes or until the cheese melts and turns golden.

Serve with a salad and a side dip such as sour cream and chives.

Traditional potato tortilla (serves four)

This recipe will make a large tortilla that will serve four to six people. It is often quite difficult for sufferers to divide portions evenly. They usually give others a large slice and themselves a smaller one. Trust someone else to divide the meal for you so that there is no risk of your eating disorder controlling the portion sizes.

Ingredients

450g (1lb) waxy potato (peeled)   4 eggs
1 large onion   Salt and pepper for seasoning
3 tablespoons vegetable oil

Chop the potatoes into very thin slices and the onion into thinly sliced rings. Heat two tablespoons of the oil in a large, heavy-based frying pan. Add the potato and the onion rings, and cook on a low heat for about ten minutes until the potatoes are soft.

Beat the four eggs together in a large bowl and season with salt and pepper. Add the partially cooked potato and onion. Heat the remaining oil in the pan and add the egg and potato mixture. Cook gently for between five and eight minutes until the mixture is nearly set.

Now it is time to turn the tortilla. Place a large plate over the pan. Turn over the pan so that the tortilla falls gently onto the plate and then slide it carefully back into the pan. Cook for a further two to three minutes until golden brown. Serve with a fresh green salad.

Savoury nut loaf (serves four)

Nuts are a good source of protein and also very healthy since they contain essential oils. Sufferers can be afraid of including nuts in their diet because they believe they contain too many calories. Remember the rule that no food is 'bad' –

all of them should be permitted. This recipe is an excellent way of reintroducing nuts back into your diet.

Ingredients

1 tablespoon olive oil
1 chopped onion
1 chopped leek
2 celery sticks (finely chopped)
225g (6oz) chopped mushrooms
425g (15oz) tin of lentils (rinsed and drained)

115g (4oz) mixed nuts (all finely chopped)
50g (2oz) self-raising flour
50g (2oz) cheddar cheese
1 medium egg (beaten)
3–4 tablespoons chopped herbs
Salt and pepper

Pre-heat the oven to 190°C / 375°F / Gas Mark 5. Lightly grease and line a large (2 lb) loaf tin with greaseproof paper. Heat the olive oil in a large saucepan and add the chopped onion, leeks, celery sticks and mushrooms.

Cook the vegetables gently for ten minutes until they are soft. Do not let them brown. Add the lentils, grated cheese, nuts and flour to the pan, as well as the beaten egg and herbs. Season with salt and pepper, and mix thoroughly.

Spoon the combined mixture into the loaf tin. Press the mixture right into the corners and level the surface. Bake for 50–60 minutes until the top is lightly brown and firm to the touch.

Cool for a few minutes in the tin and then turn out. Cut into slices and serve with potatoes and salad.

Raisin and cherry flapjack

As you progress in your recovery, you will need to add extra snacks in order to gain weight to a healthy level. It is good to include some wholesome cereal bars into your diet as these are both tasty and nutritious.

Ingredients

150g (5oz) porridge oats
115g (4oz) sugar
25g (1oz) raisins
50g (2oz) glacé cherries.

115g (4oz) polyunsaturated margarine (melted)
Oil (for greasing the baking tray)

Pre-heat the oven to 190°C / 375°F / Gas Mark 5. Grease a shallow baking tray. Stir the oats, sugar and fruit together in a bowl. Pour in the melted margarine and blend until thoroughly combined.

Press into the greased tin and bake in the oven for 15–20 minutes. Remove the tray from the oven and mark into 14 bars. Leave to cool in the tray for five minutes, then remove and place on a wire tray to cool.

Mushroom bolognese (serves four)

This dish can be made the traditional way, with minced beef. However, this vegetarian version often feels lighter and less intimidating for sufferers. Again, this meal serves four people so make sure that the portions are of equal sizes.

Ingredients

450g (1lb) fresh mushrooms
1 tablespoon oil
1 chopped onion
1 garlic clove (optional)

400 g (14oz) tin of tomatoes
15 ml (1 tablespoon) tomato paste
350g (12oz) dried pasta

Cook the dried pasta in a pan of boiling water for 10–12 minutes until tender. You can use 450 g (1 lb) of fresh pasta for this recipe if you prefer.

Clean the mushrooms and then cut them into small chunks. Heat the oil in a large pan. Add the chopped onion and garlic and cook for two to three minutes. Now add the mushrooms and continue cooking on a high heat for three to four minutes.

Stir the ingredients occasionally to prevent them sticking. Add the tomato paste and tin of tomatoes. Turn down the heat and continue to cook for five minutes. Season the mushroom sauce to taste.

Drain the cooked pasta and place in a large bowl. Add the mushroom sauce and mix together. Serve with grated Parmesan cheese and a fresh salad.

Apple and hazelnut cluster (serves four to six)

It may be that you have previously viewed desserts as unacceptable in your diet. The only time eating disorder sufferers tend to choose these higher-calorie items is during a binge and they then consider themselves 'bad' afterwards.

Desserts are allowed in a healthy diet, though, and as you progress in your recovery, you will need to start including them. It can often be easier to begin with a fruit-based dessert such as this crumble. I have used apples here since they are a particular favourite of mine, although you can substitute any fruit that you like.

For the crumble mix:

Ingredients

175g (6oz) plain flour	75g (3oz) caster sugar
75g (3oz) margarine or butter	25g (1oz) roughly chopped hazelnuts

For the filling:

Ingredients

Juice of one orange	50g (2oz) light brown sugar
450g (1lb) cooking apples	

Pre-heat the oven to 200°C / 400°F / Gas Mark 6. Butter a large baking dish. Peel and core the apples, then slice them and place in the buttered dish. Sprinkle the light brown sugar and pour the orange juice over the apples. Place this dish to one side for a moment.

Place the flour into another bowl and rub in the butter using your fingertips until the mixture resembles breadcrumbs. Stir in the sugar and nuts.

Scatter this crumble topping over the fruit and press down firmly to seal in the fruit juices. Bake in the oven for 30–35 minutes until golden brown. Serve with cream or custard.

Vegetable rice (serves two)

Rice is an extremely good source of carbohydrates. It can be cooked with a variety of vegetables or protein such as chicken or lentils. It makes a light dish which is not too filling and can be helpful for anorexia sufferers in the early stages of

Ingredients

225g (8oz) Basmati rice	50g (2oz) frozen sweetcorn
2 tablespoons oil	50g (2oz) frozen peas.
1 onion (finely chopped)	Salt
1 carrot (finely diced)	

recovery or compulsive overeaters who are learning to adjust to a lower-calorie diet.

Wash the Basmati rice in cold water. Place in a bowl and cover with fresh water. Leave to soak for 30 minutes. Heat the oil in a frying pan, add the onion and fry for five minutes. Stir in the carrot and cook for three to four minutes. Drain the rice and mix in the peas and sweetcorn.

Add all three ingredients to the pan and fry for four to five minutes. Add 475 ml (16fl oz) of vegetable stock and salt to taste. Bring to the boil and then cover the pan. Turn down the heat and simmer for 15 minutes until all the water has been absorbed. Leave to stand for ten minutes before serving.

This dish also goes well with any protein item such as an omelette.

Recipes for 'safe' and 'unsafe' foods

All eating disorder sufferers have their own personal list of 'safe' and 'unsafe' foods.

'Safe' foods are those which are very low in calories and can lead to weight loss if they are eaten exclusively. These include fruit and vegetables as well as drinks such as diet cola and water.

'Unsafe' foods are generally ones that are higher in calories and contain fat and/or sugar, such as cakes, ice cream, biscuits and savoury snacks. These are often used by bulimia sufferers and overeaters as binge foods when they can no longer maintain their regular diets.

One of the aims of this workbook is to show that there are no inherently good or bad ('safe' or 'unsafe') foods. All food types should be included in a healthy eating plan. Even foods which are higher in fat and sugar are recommended if eaten in moderation. Eating disorder sufferers usually feel intense guilt if they break their diets and eat an 'unsafe' food and this can lead to further restrictive behaviour or even self-harming.

Most sufferers do want to eat 'unsafe' foods but are too frightened by their calorie content. This often results in them denying that they even like the taste of certain higher calorie foods.

During my years as an anorexia sufferer, I especially desired chocolate. My body was starving and because it desperately required calories, I would experience strong cravings as a result. I would permit myself to buy the chocolate but, although I desperately wanted to eat it, I would hide it away in my room instead. It was an 'unsafe' food and I would not allow myself to actually eat it.

From time to time, I would get out the chocolate just to look at it. Very occasionally, I would eat some of it but almost immediately I was flooded with feelings of guilt. To try and counteract this intense emotion, I chose unhealthy coping strategies and would restrict my diet further or exercise ferociously.

Thursday 4 December 1997

I feel like the walls are closing in on me and I'm trapped in this very dark place. I want so much to escape from there and be free from all the pain. I wish I could escape the guilt I feel every time I eat. It is especially strong tonight because I ate a square of chocolate. I feel so disgusted with myself — chocolate is a forbidden food. I'm not allowed to have it because I'm not a good person. I know that I do things wrong all of the time and I'm certain everyone hates me.

Saturday 2 December 2000

Simon and I went out for a meal tonight. We went to a little Italian bistro just round the corner. It was so lovely. The restaurant was decorated with Christmas lights and there were candles burning everywhere. We had a delicious meal — pasta with tomato and basil sauce served with a side salad. Then together we had a large chocolate dessert made for sharing. It was wonderful. I've never tasted chocolate like it and I really enjoyed it. I didn't feel guilty at all. In fact I've only just realized it but I'm not counting calories any more. I couldn't even begin to work out how much I ate tonight and I don't care. It was a lovely meal and that's all that matters.

There are healthy ways of introducing 'unsafe' foods into your diet without harming yourself. Start by making a list of the foods that you feel are 'unsafe'.

Exercise 18.1

My 'unsafe' foods

_____

_____

_____

_____

_____

_____

_____

_____

Normal eating involves gradually incorporating all the foods you have discarded as 'unsafe'. This means that in time you will need to include them in your daily eating plan.

When selecting the 'unsafe' food, it is important to select a normal-sized portion. If you are choosing crisps, for example, buy a standard 30g (individual) packet. Do not buy a family-sized bag and select a few crisps as your portion. When you suffer from an eating disorder, it is hard to judge portion sizes accurately. If necessary, use a set of scales to ensure that you are eating a full portion. As an anorexia sufferer, my judgement in this area was very poor. I would think I had cut a 20g (less than 1oz) piece of cheese but when I actually weighed it, I would find that it was only 10g (less than half an ounce).

It is likely that you will feel guilty after you have eaten an 'unsafe' food. This is a good time to use distraction techniques. Have an activity planned to distract your train of thought. Remember that the feelings of guilt will pass but only if you continue to fight on with your recovery by constantly challenging the eating disorder.

Finally, do not forget to reward yourself each time you have broken the rigid rules that you have set. This does not need to be an expensive treat. Remember to make certain that all rewards and treats are non-food-related.

Reintroducing 'unsafe foods' into your diet can be a difficult process and the exercises below may help you to break the pattern of restriction.

Exercise 18.2

Lucky dip

Put a selection of 'safe' and 'unsafe' foods into a covered container. Shake the container and reach in and pull out an item. You are not allowed to look in the container or feel the shapes of the items within. It must be a totally random test. (If you feel unable to do this yourself, ask a friend to help.) Your task is then to eat the item whether it is 'safe' or 'unsafe'.

Begin by trying this experiment once a week but gradually increase the frequency until you are completing it once a day.

Exercise 18.3

My 1–10 of unsafe foods

List all of your 'unsafe' foods in order, starting with the safest at number 1 and moving up to the most intimidating at number 10.

Start with number 1 and draw up a plan for incorporating this into your diet. If your 'unsafe' food is also a binge food, you may be concerned that it could trigger a binge or vomit episode. If this is the case, plan to eat the food in company so that you are unable to binge once you have eaten your allocated portion.

If eating with a friend feels too stressful, try eating on your own in a public place such a coffee shop. The presence of other customers will make it extremely difficult to binge.

Work out when is best for trying new types of food. Some people prefer to carry out this exercise early in the day since they are too tired by the evening when it can all seem too stressful. You choose the time of day that works best for you. Remember that you are in control of your own recovery.

Recipes for social eating

Sufferers often find it extremely difficult to eat in company. They feel that they are being watched and become self-conscious about their unusual behaviours. It can therefore be helpful for recovering sufferers to eat with people who do not have eating disorders. It shows them that it is possible to feel comfortable around food.

Eating is just a necessary human function which should be automatic when a person is hungry. As mentioned earlier, sufferers frequently employ specific ritual ways of eating (such as one pea or bean at a time). It is far harder to perform these rituals in public since other diners may notice the strange patterns of behaviour.

When you are trying to break these routines, it can be helpful to make sure that you have companions (such as a trusted friend or relative) with you during mealtimes. Try to eat at a similar speed to the other diners since this also makes it harder to carry out any food rituals.

Side dishes

When I met Simon, I had not eaten a meal in a restaurant for a number of years and I found the prospect quite daunting. One of my greatest fears was being presented with a heaped plate of food.

We avoided this problem by ordering a selection of side dishes and sharing them between us. I would pick and choose which items I wanted and at no point did they appear heaped on one plate. I found that I actually ate a lot more this way because the panic and paralysing fear were removed by this approach. I felt more relaxed and was able to eat until I felt full.

The teaspoon test

Sufferers often feel afraid to experiment with new foods because they are concerned about how much they will have to eat. During my anorexia, I wanted to try certain desserts or cakes but felt unable to order a whole portion for myself. A trusted friend or relative can help you with this activity.

Ask the friend to order or buy a dessert or cake. When it arrives, allow yourself to try some using a teaspoon. If you like the taste (remember that you must be totally honest here) then share the item with your friend. Even if you have just one extra teaspoon, this is progress.

Cooking for others

Both anorexia and bulimia sufferers often feel a need to be around food – looking at it, touching it and cooking with it – although not actually eating it. Eating disorder sufferers often cook many of the meals for their family and friends as a result. I used to enjoy making cakes and biscuits in particular. Sufferers may also be interested in cooking programmes and look out for recipes in magazines.

The main problem is that they feel a need to be around food since their body is starving but they cannot allow themselves to enjoy the food that they have prepared. The best they can do is vicariously enjoy their meals by watching others eat them. They may even question their family during and after each meal to find out exactly how it tasted.

This activity recognizes that cooking only for others (and not yourself) is a symptom of the illness and needs to be stopped. Sufferers are still allowed to cook meals and snacks but they first have to agree to join in with the eating too. Every time they cook for others, they must have a serving of the food as well.

As with most of the activities and exercises in this book, start gently and gradually increase your portion until you are having a full plate of food as well. Begin with a quarter-portion and stay at this level for a week. Then move on to a half-portion, followed by three-quarters and finally a full portion. Cooking can be a fun hobby but it is important to be able to enjoy your hard work too.

Conclusion:
The Jigsaw Approach to Recovery

It may be that you have just started writing a thoughts and feelings diary or have begun to practise CBT and feel that another approach (such as exposure therapy) is too complicated. Do not dismiss a new therapeutic approach until you have given it a chance. I am certain that my own recovery succeeded because I was willing to try each new type of therapy that was suggested to me until I had learnt which approaches worked best in my own case.

People sometimes say that in order to recover, you must adhere to just one type of therapy. I do not agree. Often, an illness has many different components and one type of therapy is not necessarily appropriate for every aspect of the disorder. I like to think of it as a 'jigsaw approach to recovery'.

I used CBT to help build up my self-esteem, whereas exposure therapy worked best for me when it came to eating a normal diet again. My thoughts and feelings diaries helped me to deal with memories of abuse, whereas using emotional distance worked best for coping with the negative people in my life.

All these different therapies were essential for me to make a full recovery. Find out what works best for you and develop your own individual jigsaw to help you complete your recovery.

Eating disorders cause a great deal of physical and mental damage. When you are suffering from one of these illnesses, it can often feel like a life sentence. However, recovery is not only possible – it is a very realistic goal. You may experience some problems along the way but the reward is a chance to regain your life and to have a happy, healthy future. I would like to take this opportunity to wish you the best of luck with your own recovery.

Useful Resources

Eating disorder associations (worldwide)

Anorexia Nervosa and Related Eating Disorders Inc. (ANRED)
(USA)
E-mail: jarinor@rio.com
Website: www.anred.com

BEAT
First Floor
Wensum House
103 Prince of Wales Road
Norwich NR1 1DW
Telephone Helpline: 0845 634 1414 (10.30 am – 8.30 pm weekdays)
Youth Helpline: 0845 634 7650 (4.30 pm – 8.30 pm weekdays)
Support E-mail: help@b-eat.co.uk
Beat Youthline E-mail: fyp@b-eat.co.uk
Website: www.b-eat.co.uk

British Columbia Eating Disorders Association
526 Michigan Street
Victoria
BC
Canada
V8V 1S2
Tel: 00 1 250 383 2755 or 00 1 250 383 5518
Website: webhome.idirect.com/~bceda/index.html

Eating Disorders Association

PO Box 80
142 Green Bay
Auckland 7
New Zealand
Tel: 00 64 9 818 9561
Fax: 00 64 9 818 9568
E-mail: anorexia@xtra.co.nz

Eating Disorders Association (Queensland)

225 Logan Road
Woollongabba
4102 (Australia)
Australia
Tel: 00 61 7 3891 3660
Fax: 00 61 7 3891 3662
Crisis counselling numbers:
Lifeline: 131114
Kids Helpline: 1800 551800
Parents Helpline: 1300 301 300
E-mail: admin@eda.org.au
Website: www.eda.org.au/home.htm

National Association of Anorexia Nervosa and Associated Disorders (ANAD)

PO Box 7
Highland Park
IL 60035
USA
Tel: 00 1 847 831 3438
E-mail: anad20@aol.com
Website: www.anad.org

Somerset & Wessex Eating Disorders Association (SWEDA)
Strode House
10 Leigh Road
Street
Somerset
UK
Support Telephone Helpline: 01458 448600 (10 am – 1 pm Wednesdays; 4 pm – 7 pm Thursdays)
E-mail: support@swedauk.org
Website: www.swedauk.org

Other useful organizations

Childline (UK)
Tel: 0800 1111 (Open 24 hours a day, seven days a week)
Website: www.childline.org.uk

Rape Crisis Federation (UK)
E-mail: info@rapecrisis.co.uk
Website: www.rapecrisis.co.uk

The Samaritans (UK)
Tel: 08457 909090 (UK) or 1850 609090 (Republic of Ireland) (help 24 hours a day)
E-mail: jo@samaritans.org
Website: www.samaritans.org.uk

Victim Support (UK)
Cranmer House
39 Brixton Road
London SW9 6DZ
Tel: 020 7735 9166
Fax: 020 7582 5712
E-mail: Contact@victimsupport.org.uk
Website: www.victimsupport.org.uk

Index

abdominal breathing 143
acid reflux 32
addiction
    to exercise 24, 179
    to vomiting 116–17
adrenaline 138, 139, 141
adulthood, fear of 53–4
'advantages' of eating
    disorders 28–9, 39–42,
    46–53
aerobic exercise 179
affirmations 104–5, 107–8,
    186–7
aggression 129, 148, 149,
    152–3, 156
alcohol abuse 33
'all or nothing' thinking 105
anaemia 30
anger 31, 69, 115, 124,
    127–36, 148
    calming your 128, 129–36
    expression 127, 128–9
    and fear 135, 136
    recognising your reasons
        for feeling 130–1, 132
    suppression 127, 129
anorexia nervosa 10–13
    characteristics of 17–18
    and clothing choice 100
    co-occurrence with
        bulimia 19, 23–4
    co-occurrence with
        obsessive compulsive
        disorder 97–8
    competitiveness of 94
    deaths from 31
    definition 15–18
    diagnosis 16
    diet plans for 62, 196
    dreams and 109–10
    dysfunctional beliefs of
        103, 105
    and fear of adulthood
        53–4
    and food shopping 59

'functions' of 29
gender bias in 16
health dangers of 30–1
and hospitalization 11,
    12, 53
and hunger 61, 113–14
and identity 44
and negative automatic
    thoughts 73–4
and overexercising 121–2,
    179
and passivity 154
and perfectionism 160–1
physical impact 30
psychological impact
    30–1
and reaching a healthy
    body weight 175
reasons for the
    development of 17,
    53–4
recognising you are
    underweight 176–8
recovery 39–43
risk factors for 16–17
and social eating 210
and 'unsafe' foods 206–8
antidepressants 9–10
anxiety 84, 115, 137–45, 165
    of bulimia nervosa 34
    combating through
        exposure therapy
        86–90
    definition 137–9
    and the 'fight or flight'
        reaction 137, 138
    honesty regarding 141
    internal thoughts of 137
    learning to understand
        the process of 140
    physical feelings of 137,
        138
    triggers 139, 140
Apple and Hazelnut Cluster
    (recipe) 204–5

arrhythmia 31
assertiveness 146–57
    advantages of 156
    characteristics of 149
    disadvantages of 156
    don'ts 150–3
    dos 149–50
attractiveness
    male views on 50
    purposefully destroying
        your 176
automatic thoughts see
    negative automatic
    thoughts
avoidance behaviour 139

beliefs, dysfunctional
    103–12
    common 104
    dreams/nightmares
        109–12
    and 'the voice' 104–9,
        110
    writing down your 104
binge eating 19, 31–4, 209
    and anger 127
    calorie intake during 19,
        114
    of compulsive overeating
        21–2
    daily eating plans for 61
    distraction techniques for
        63
    emotional reasons for
        115
    and food shopping 59–60
    health dangers of 31–4
    physical reasons for
        113–15
    putting an end to 113–16
    and reaching a healthy
        body weight 175
    urge to 60
binge eating disorder see
    compulsive overeating

binge/fast cycle 114
blame 161–2
    self-blame 10, 80–1, 106
bleeding, internal 32
blood sugar levels 47
    low 34
body
    distorted view of 31
    hiding emaciation 16, 100
body dysmorphia 15, 24
body image
    distortion/dissatisfactio
    n 16, 176
body types 26–7, 175
body weight *see* weight
Bolognese, Mushroom
    (recipe) 204
bone density, loss of 30, 41
boredom 115
bowel, lazy 31
breakfasts 175, 194–5,
    199–200
breathing techniques
    129–30, 131, 133, 142–3
bulimarexia 15, 23–4
bulimia nervosa 15
    and anger 127
    binge/fast cycle of 114
    calorie intake during 19
    characteristics of 20–1
    co-occurrence with
        anorexia 19, 23–4
    competitiveness of 94
    deaths from 31, 32
    definition 18–21
    diet plans for 196
    and feelings of fullness
        61
    and food shopping
        59–60, 116
    gender bias of 19
    health dangers of 31–5
    and hunger 113–14
    and malnourishment 192
    and overexercising 121–2
    physical impact 31–4
    psychological impact
        34–5
    and reaching a healthy
        body weight 175
    reasons for the
        development of 19

recovery from 19
bulking agents 120
bullying 14, 151, 153

calories
    counting 98, 178, 196
    daily requirements 196
    eating foods with
        unknown levels of
        65–6
    intake during binge
        episodes 19, 114
    low-calorie foods 191
    plan for increasing your
        intake 45
    requirements for weight
        gain 58
carbohydrates 175
catastrophic thinking 79
cathartic colon 31
CBT *see* cognitive behaviour
    therapy
celebrities, stick-thin 181–2
challenges 65–6
Cheese and Potato Fritters
    (recipe) 197
Cheese and Tomato Potato
    Wedges (recipe) 201–2
Cherry and Raisin Flapjack
    (recipe) 203–4
chest pain 33
childhood abuse 9–11, 68,
    109, 161
'chipmunk cheeks' 32
chocolate 206–7
chronic fatigue syndrome 10
clothing
    over-large 16, 100
    sizes 176–8, 185
cognitive behaviour therapy
    (CBT) 72–85, 95, 115,
    118, 124, 212
    and anger management
        130, 131–2
    and anxiety management
        141
    challenging negativity
        with 77–82
    and confusing thoughts
        and feelings 76–7

four-column thoughts
    and moods charts
    75–6, 77
and learning to accept
    compliments 180
and negative thoughts
    72–85
six-column thoughts and
    moods charts 82–3
to combat 'voices' 104–5
comedy 171–2
comfort foods 113, 114
community mental health
    teams 11
comparison-making 177,
    192
competitiveness 94, 158
compliments 40, 173, 180–1
compulsive overeating
    (binge eating disorder)
    15, 21–3
    bingeing of 21–2
    causes of 22
    characteristics of 22–3
    'constant nibblers' 22
    diagnosis 21–2
    diet plans for 196
    and feelings of fullness
        61
    and food shopping 60
    health dangers of 35–6
    and reaching a healthy
        body weight 175
compulsive overexercising
    (activity disorder) 24
concentration difficulties 31,
    34
confidence building 167–72
conflict avoidance 148
constipation 30, 33, 119,
    120
constructive criticism 150
control issues 13, 16, 21, 48,
    70, 95–6, 188
    of bulimarexia 24
    taking back control 85
cooking for others 210–11
coping methods, eating
    disorders as 15, 28–9,
    39–40, 48, 49, 51–2
cravings 114–15

crumbles, Apple and Hazelnut (recipe) 204–5
cutting behaviours 11

daily eating plans 60–2, 194–6
dangerous behaviours 30–6, 113–26
deadness 124
death
    dreams about 110–11
    due to eating disorders 31, 32
decision-making difficulties 35
defining eating disorders 15–27
dehydration 19, 31, 33
denial 106
dental health 32
depression 9, 19, 171
    and anorexia 31
    and bulimarexia 24
    and bulimia nervosa 34
    and compulsive overeating 22
    and perfectionism 158
desserts 203–5
diaries
    binge eating 115
    thoughts and feelings 67–71, 212
    to put an end to vomiting 117–18
diet plans 60–2, 194–6
diets 61, 91–2
dinners/lunches 194–5, 197–203, 204, 205–6
disadvantages of eating disorders 52–3
distorted thoughts 73
distraction techniques 62–5, 66, 118, 124, 144–5
diuretics 18
    giving up 113, 114, 121
dizziness 30, 37
doctors
    appointments 133
    and giving up laxatives 119–20
dreams 68–9, 109–12
drug abuse 33

eating
    emotional 22
    healthy 94, 95
    time spent on 100–1
    see also binge eating
eating disorders not otherwise specified (ED-NOS) 23–6
eating plans 60–2, 194–6
ectomorphs 26
egg dishes (recipes) 191
    Low-fat Omelette 199–200
    Scrambled Eggs 200–1
    Traditional Potato Tortilla 202
electrolyte imbalance 31, 33, 121
emetics 32
emetophobia 25
emotional eating 22
endomorphs 26
endorphins 24, 171
energy levels 178
epilepsy 32
essay writing 160
evening classes 170
exposure therapy 86–90, 141, 212
    extinction 86
    flooding 86, 89
    graded/graduated exposure 86, 89
    group therapy 88
    habituation 86
    hierarchies of fear 86–7
    for panic attacks 88–9
    patient-directed 87
    results of 89–90
    tasks for 90
    therapist-assisted 87–8
    virtual/imaginal exposure 86, 89–90
    in vivo exposure 86
extinction 86
eye problems 33

failure 40, 70
family relationships, difficult 9–13, 68–9, 158, 161–4, 181
family therapy 12, 13, 161

'fat feelings' 42
fatigue/tiredness 30, 32, 33
fear 105
    of adulthood 53–4
    and anger 135, 136
    challenging your 78
    facing 54, 86–90
    of failure 40
    of food 16, 25
    identifying your 54, 55
    and perfectionism 160
    of recovery 173
    of the symptoms of fear ('the second fear') 142
    of weight gain 16, 17, 48–9
feather exercise 142
feelings 59
    difference to thoughts 76–7
    thoughts and feelings diaries 67–71
    thoughts and moods charts 75–6, 77, 82–3
fibre 120–1
'fight or flight' reaction 137, 138
Flapjack, Raisin and Cherry (recipe) 203–4
flooding 86, 89
food
    anxiety about 139
    as 'bad' 58, 110
    comfort 113, 114
    disliked 193–4
    fear of 16, 25
    as healthy 58, 59
    hiding 11
    'impossible' 68, 69–70
    intimidating 191
    introducing new 65–6, 90, 179, 190, 209, 210
    low-calorie 191
    as medicine 190
    obsessions 10, 17, 47
    for recovery 190–4
    restricting certain types of 24–5
    rituals 98, 209
    'safe' 206, 208, 209
    shopping for 59–60, 88, 116, 133–4

with unknown calories
65–6
'unsafe' 59, 60, 88, 179,
206–9
food groups 114
food-combining 193
Fritters, Cheese and Potato
(recipe) 197
fullness, feelings of 61
fun, learning to have 170
functions of eating
disorders 28–9, 39–42,
46–53

games, mental 144–5
'grazing', between meals 22,
90
guilt 10–11, 17, 51, 95, 114,
153, 206–8
of bulimarexia 23
of bulimia 18, 19, 20
coping with 58–66
and recovery 41
and self-harm 123, 124

habituation 86
hair
lanugo 30
loss 30
hallucinations 9–10
happiness 70–1
Hazelnut and Apple Cluster
(recipe) 204–5
headaches 33
health dangers 30–6, 113–26
healthcare professionals
sharing your thoughts
with 67
see also doctors
healthy eating 94, 95
heart problems 31, 32
heart rate 30, 31
help, asking for 115
high-achievers 16–17
honesty 67–8, 69–70, 141
hospitalization 11, 12, 53
food and 94, 193–4
humour 132
hunger 41, 47, 52, 58, 174
and bingeing 113–15
denial of 61

and food shopping 59
recognition 56
hypoglycaemia 34

identity, 'eating disorder' 44,
173, 178
insomnia 30
International Emetophobia
Society 25
irritability 31

jacket potatoes 191
jumping to conclusions 106

kidney damage 33

labelling 106
lanugo hair 30
large intestine, lazy 119
laughter 171–2
laxatives 19, 114
giving up 45, 63, 113,
114, 118–21
health dangers of 31–2
letter writing, to your eating
disorder 57
lies 48, 123
life stresses, coping with 80,
124–6, 133–4
lifestyle 141
light sensitivity 30
listening exercise 144
loss 123
Low-fat Omelette (recipe)
199–200
lunches/dinners 194–5,
197–203, 204, 205–6

magazines 92–4, 181–2
magnesium 32
malnutrition 25, 192
Mashed Potatoes (recipe)
201
ME (chronic fatigue
syndrome) 10
meals
regular 114
small but regular 192
media 92–4, 181–2
memory problems 34

men, and eating disorders
19, 22
menstruation
cessation 16, 33, 41, 53,
94
and cravings 114
irregular 33
mental games 144–5
mesomorphs 26
metabolic rate 33
milk substitutes 193
'mind reading' 106
mind-sets, negative 72
mirrors, compulsive
checking in 101
misunderstandings 132
models 92–4
mood swings 134
mouth ulcers 33
muscle cramps 33
mushrooms (recipes)
Bolognese 204
Stuffed 198–9
myths about eating
disorders 44–5, 46–52

needs
identification 146–8
satisfaction 156–7
needs form 156–7
negative automatic thoughts
73–85
challenging 76–85
definition 73–5, 77
recording 75–7
negative behaviour, and
negative thoughts 72
negative influences 56
negative outlooks 70–1
negative thoughts
and anxiety 139, 141, 144
automatic 72–85
catastrophic 79
nightmares 68–9, 109–12
no, learning to say 164
noise sensitivity 30
non-specific eating disorders
25–6
noticing exercise 145
numbness 124
Nut Loaf, Savoury (recipe)
202–3

obesity 22, 35–6
obsessive behaviours 34, 90
obsessive compulsive
    disorder (OCD) 25,
    97–8, 158
occupational therapists 10
oedema 30
oesophageal damage 32
omelettes 191
    Low-fat (recipe) 199–200
orthorexia 15, 24–5
osteoporosis 30, 41
other people
    cooking for 210–11
    understanding of 49
    see also social support
over-the-counter (OTC)
    medications 36
overexercising 18, 70
    compulsive (activity
        disorder) 24
    plan for decreasing 45
    stopping 63, 113, 114,
        121–2
overweight people 175–6
    see also obesity

panic attacks 34, 88–9,
    141–2
panic disorders 158
parents, problem 9–13, 158,
    161–4, 181
passive aggression 129
passivity 150–1, 153, 156
pasta, Mushroom Bolognese
    (recipe) 204
patience 141
people-pleasers 158–9, 161,
    164
perfectionism 79, 98,
    158–66, 184
    clinical/dysfunctional
        158, 159
    identifying your 160–4
    positive 158
    and rule breaking 165
    and setting time limits
        165
    and sharing imperfection
        165
    at work 164

persecutory feelings 111,
    130
personal freedom 13
personal responsibility,
    exaggerated sense of
    80–1, 107, 161
phobias 25, 140
physical exercise 115, 145,
    179–80
    extreme forms of 180
    see also overexercising
pica 25
pill, the 33
Pizzas, Vegetarian Mini
    (recipe) 197–8
Porridge, Raisin and
    Cinnamon (recipe) 199
portion sizes 208
positive affirmations 104–5,
    107–8, 186–7
'positive' aspects of eating
    disorders 28–9, 39–42,
    46–53
positive influences 56
positive qualities, identifying
    your 167–70, 182–3
potassium 31, 192
potatoes (recipes)
    Cheese and Potato
        Fritters 197
    Cheese and Tomato
        Potato Wedges 201–2
    jacket 191
    Mashed Potatoes 201
    Traditional Potato
        Tortilla 202
pregnancy 33
prejudice 36
prescription medications 36
problem-solving 124–6
progressive muscle
    relaxation 143
protein 192–3
psychiatric nurses 10–12
public situations 154
purging (by taking laxatives)
    18, 114
    distraction techniques for
        63
    inefficacy of 19

Raisin and Cherry Flapjack
    (recipe) 203–4
Raisin and Cinnamon
    Porridge (recipe) 199
rape 176
reasoning, inductive 106
recipes 197–206
    Apple and Hazelnut
        Cluster 204–5
    Bolognese, Mushroom
        204
    Cheese and Potato
        Fritters 197
    Cheese and Tomato
        Potato Wedges 201–2
    Cherry and Raisin
        Flapjack 203–4
    crumbles, Apple and
        Hazelnut 204–5
    egg dishes
        Low-fat Omelette
            199–200
        Scrambled Eggs 200–1
        Traditional Potato
            Tortilla 202
    Flapjack, Raisin and
        Cherry 203–4
    Fritters, Cheese and
        Potato 197
    Hazelnut and Apple
        Cluster 204–5
    jacket potatoes 191
    Low-fat Omelette
        199–200
    Mashed Potatoes 201
    mushrooms
        Bolognese 204
        Stuffed 198–9
    Nut Loaf, Savoury
        202–3
    omelettes 191
        Low-fat 199–200
    pasta, Mushroom
        Bolognese 204
    Pizzas, Vegetarian Mini
        197–8
    Porridge, Raisin and
        Cinnamon 199
    potatoes
        Cheese and Potato
            Fritters 197

Cheese and Tomato
Potato Wedges
201–2
jacket 191
Mashed Potatoes 201
Traditional Potato
Tortilla 202
Raisin and Cherry
Flapjack 203–4
Raisin and Cinnamon
Porridge 199
Rice, Vegetable 205–6
Savoury Nut Loaf
202–3
Scrambled Eggs 200–1
Stuffed Mushrooms
198–9
Vegetable Rice 205–6
Vegetarian Mini Pizzas
197–8

recovery
assessing your feelings
about 173, 174
benefits of 28, 36–9
choosing 15, 28–43
conditional 43
and controlling your
negative automatic
thoughts 85
design for 45
difficulties
surrounding/feeling in
two minds about 15,
28–9, 39–43, 44–57,
173
and the eating disorder as
your friend myth 44–5
farewell letters for 57
foods for 190–4
full 188–9
goals of 37–9
guilt and 59
jigsaw approach to 212
motivation for 37–9,
52–3
negative influences on 56
positive influences on 56
as slow process 45, 189
timetable 45–54
see also setbacks; weight,
healthy, living at

relapses 184
relaxation techniques 131,
141, 142–5
repetition exercise 144
responsibility, exaggerated
sense of 80–1, 107, 161
Rice, Vegetable (recipe)
205–6
risk taking 40
rituals 34, 98, 100–1, 209
role reversal exercise 64–5
role-plays 180–1
romantic relationships 13
routines 90
rules
of eating disorders 96–7,
98, 99, 105
perfectionist 165
setting 106

salivary glands, swollen 32
sandwiches, open 191
Savoury Nut Loaf (recipe)
202–3
Scrambled Eggs (recipe)
200–1
secretiveness 16, 18–20
self-acceptance 181–3
self-blame 10, 80–1, 106
self-care 181–3
self-confidence 163
self-criticism 79
self-esteem
boosting 12, 156
issues 10, 13, 16, 19,
36–7, 68, 72–3, 151,
158–9, 161, 163,
180–1
resilient 148
self-harming 10, 11, 109,
206
definition 123
distraction techniques for
63
and emotional pain 122,
123
giving up 113, 122–6
as self-punishment 123,
124
triggers 123–4
self-hatred 181, 207
self-help groups 170, 181

self-inflicted violence (SIV)
see self-harm
self-love 181–3
self-praise 168
self-punishment 51, 95, 123,
124, 130
self-talk 72, 79
positive 130
selflessness 107
Seneca 132–3
setbacks 184–9
analysing your 187–8
coping strategies for
184–6
positive affirmations for
186–7
sex drive, diminished/lost
30
sexual abuse 176
sexual harassment 10
shame 18, 19, 50, 67, 116
shoplifting 19
sibling rivalry 69, 162–3
'sick role' 40, 42
side dishes 210
size, assessing your true
176–8
skin 30, 32
sleep disruption 35
slimming drugs 32–3, 36
snacks 194–5
'snack pots' 191–2
social eating 209–10
social situations 155
social support 170
networks of 181
for tackling negative
thoughts 81–2
to combat bingeing
115–16
to combat vomiting 116,
118
to stop negative
behaviours 63
when food shopping 60
social withdrawal/isolation
16, 31, 34, 35, 36, 90
sore throats 33
soya products 193
stomach
damage to 32
delayed emptying 32

stress 141
Stuffed Mushrooms (recipe) 198–9
subconscious mind 111
subjective units of distress scale (SUDS) 87
suicidal feelings 11, 24, 34
suicide, completed 31
systemic desensitization (graded/graduated exposure) 86, 89

'talking things through' 132
target-setting 125, 126
teeth, damage to 32
telephone calls 90
thoughts
    awareness of your 84–5
    difference to feelings 76–7
    and mood 84
    negative 72–85, 139, 141, 144
thoughts and feelings diaries 67–71
thoughts and moods charts
    four-column 75–6, 77
    six-column 82–3
tidiness 98
time rituals 100–1
Traditional Potato Tortilla (recipe) 202
treats 171
trembling 32, 37
triggers (eating disorder) 91–102, 184–5
    challenging your 94–5
    definition 91–2
    listing your 92, 93
    self-harming 123–4
types of eating disorders 15–26

ulcers, mouth 33
underweight state, recognition 176–8
unhappiness 51–2
unlovable feelings 109, 110, 146

Vegetable Rice (recipe) 205–6
Vegetarian Mini Pizzas (recipe) 197–8
vegetarianism 192–3
victim role 85
visualization 39, 108–9, 131
vitamin and mineral supplements 192
'voice, the' (of your eating disorder) 70, 104–9, 110
vomiting 18, 114
    and anger 127
    blood 32
    of bulimarexia 23
    and dehydration 19, 31, 33
    fear of 25
    health dangers of 31–3
    inefficacy of 19
    stopping 113, 116–18

water intake 120–1
water retention 30, 119, 120, 121
weakness 30, 32
weighing yourself 92
    compulsive 45, 99
weight 16
    constantly shifting targets 96
    dramatic fluctuation 33
    ideal 173–6, 179
    living at a healthy level 173–83
    yo-yo 175
    see also obesity; overweight people; underweight state
weight charts 174
weight gain
    calorie requirements for 58
    fear of 16, 17, 48–9
    intimidating prospect of 173
    water-based 119, 120
weight loss 30, 196
Wharton, Edith 166
work 155
    bullying at 10

negative automatic thoughts at 81
perfectionism at 164
'worst-case scenario' thinking 79–80, 106
writing things down 57, 104, 160, 188
    see also diaries

yoga 179–80